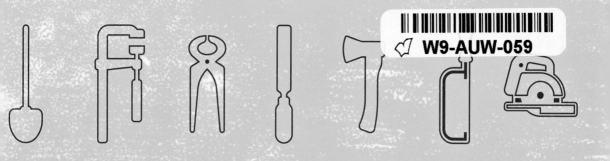
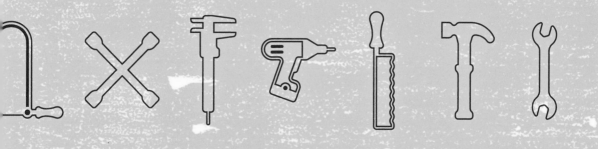
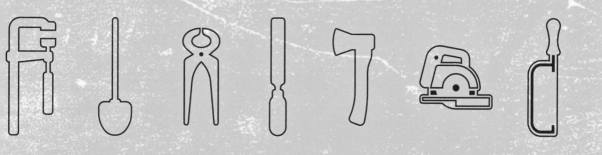
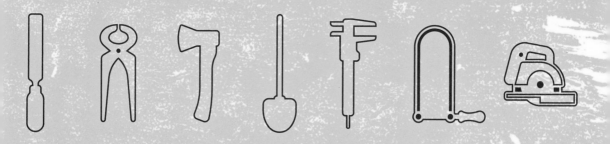

POPULAR MECHANICS

THE ULTIMATE TOOL BOOK

HEARST
books

CONTENTS

FOREWORD 005

BEFORE YOU BEGIN 006

🔧 **CONSTRUCTION** 011

🪛 **WOODWORKING** 087

🔨 **LANDSCAPING** 141

🔧 **MECHANICAL** 175

INDEX 236

PHOTO CREDITS 239

FOREWORD

When faced with something broken, *Popular Mechanics* readers aren't the type to worry. Instead we roll up our sleeves and fix the problem. Since the magazine started in 1902, *Popular Mechanics* has been all about self-sufficiency. About knowledge and experience. But also about willingness—willingness to learn and ask questions and, most important, try.

We put this book together for people who hate to give up and who always think they can do things themselves. It's a foundation of real knowledge based on more than a hundred years of providing expertise for nearly every DIY project you may encounter in your life. A definitive guide to the most important tools you can own, this book will give you more than inspiration. It will give you confidence.

At a time when fewer and fewer people actually know how to make and do things, by picking up this book you have made a commitment to taking care of yourself. You want to handle the issues that arise with owning a car, a home, a lawn you're not ashamed of. And when you find something you don't know how to do, you want to learn.

There are big rewards to knowing not only how to attack what needs doing but also what tools will help you get the job done. You'll discover yourself turning to this book for everything. There's something deeply satisfying about knowing you will be able to rise to the challenge of a leaky faucet, a decrepit front stoop, or a great tree without a tree house. You're ready. It's time to get your tools in order.

—***The Editors*** of *Popular Mechanics*

BEFORE YOU BEGIN

t's highly unlikely that this is the first page you turned to in this book. The other pages are a lot more fun, as is learning about the tools on those pages. For instance, do track saws cut as smoothly and accurately as the manufacturers claim? (They do. They're fantastic, and the plunging mechanism is very handy when you want to cut a hinged top to a window seat out of a single sheet of plywood.) Maybe you've flipped the pages searching for reciprocating saws and are hoping to see if they've made any improvements on the classic you keep in the garage. (They have. You won't be disappointed.) Then, some of you might take an interest in learning about low-angle block planes. They're a surefire, low-tech tool that can't be beat.

One thing we should cop to right now: Even though this book is called *The Ultimate Tool Book*, this is still an abridged list. You can always use more tools. At least, you can always *want* more tools. But we do stand by this idea: In a lifetime of everyday projects, these hundred tools are the ones you really need.

There's simply no way to include every tool you might ever find a need for. We've left out niche tools (like a construction calculator, to help you lay out stairs or rafters quickly and with dead-on accuracy). You won't find a section on laser measurers or digital tapes—even though they're cool and are a must-have for any gadgethead. We've also neglected to talk about jacks or lifts of any kind. Nor will you find an oil filter wrench or feeler gauge for gapping spark plugs. It's not that these tools aren't handy, but we're focusing on setting a solid foundation of tools you'll use frequently. For anything else, you'll just need to make sure you have a good neighbor.

Before getting too far ahead of ourselves, we've got to consider a few things. You can probably recall the shop safety maxim Norm Abram repeated at the beginning of every episode of *The New Yankee Workshop*. To that end, we've compiled a list of safety equipment and other supplies you'll need along with your new tools. Before you start on any project, be sure your workshop is stocked with these.

Safety Equipment

FIRST AID KIT
This is one tool we hope you'll never have to use but that's crucial to have nearby. You should have gauze, sterile bandages, adhesive bandages, hydrogen peroxide, tweezers, a magnifying glass, topical antibiotic ointment, tissues, cotton swabs, burn ointment, and some white medical tape.

FIRE EXTINGUISHER
We hope you never have to use this tool, either, but it should be within reach at all times. Make sure your extinguisher is ABC rated and pressurized. If you ever do need to use it, aim it at the base of the flame and spray side to side to extinguish the fire. If you are working in a garage or basement shop, be sure to always have a clear evacuation plan in mind as well.

Supplies

 DUCT TAPE
There's a reason why one of our other books is titled *When Duct Tape Just Isn't Enough*. There's so much you can do with it, and it's great for temporary repairs, but it's not a long-term fix.

 FIVE-GALLON BUCKET
Not only is this a great tool tote, but it also doubles as a seat, a collection basin when you need to drain a plugged sink, and an impromptu stepladder.

 SANDPAPER
You'll want to keep several different grits and makes around. Garnet is soft and a terrific choice for final sanding on soft woods, but for metal, you'll be better served grabbing a sheet of silicon carbide. When stripping layers of paint, a ceramic-tooth sandpaper will tear through old, hardened coats.

 GLUE
You'll need adhesives to get some work done. While working with plumbing, the two-part primer and adhesive to run a PVC drain line is necessary. Type II carpenter's glue is a nontoxic, inexpensive, weather-resistant, all-purpose wood glue. A bottle of superglue is terrific for some everyday repairs, with its quick-drying, super-strong hold. Superglue shouldn't be used on porous materials, since it's absorbed too quickly. Gel-style superglues are easier to work with, because they're thicker and there's less runoff. It's also easier to see exactly where the glue has been applied.

For many jobs, a polyurethane glue, like Gorilla Glue, will solve many of your problems; it's extremely strong and sticks to a variety of surfaces. The caveats to

> **TIP!** To help glue last longer in the bottle, squeeze out all the air before sealing the cap.

polyurethane glue are that it can be fatal if swallowed, it will stain your skin, and its expansion rate is generally 3:1, which can be difficult to estimate. For some specialty items, you'll find the manufacturer's proprietary adhesives to be the best choice.

SPRAY LUBE

An assortment of spray lubricants should be in everyone's toolbox. Some penetrate rust; others act as a general lubricant; some leave behind a dry film that resists accumulating dust and dirt. Choose the right ones for you.

SCREWS

An array of screws will keep you working. But don't rely solely on drywall screws. Contrary to popular belief, these are not the end-all fastener. In fact, you should use them only on drywall and keep a good selection of specialty screws for your woodworking needs. Most hardware stores have an array of screws designed especially for trim work, decking, and general wood fastening. Unless it's for aesthetic reasons, you should avoid using a Phillips-head and opt for either a square drive or star drive. These latter head designs offer more points of contact and a more equal distribution of torque, which lower the chance of stripping a screw's head.

NAILS

Like screws, one type of nail doesn't work for every application. Common nails are terrific for framing, and hot-dipped galvanized commons are a smart choice for outdoor applications, like framing decks and working with cedar. Finishing nails, roofing nails, underlayment nails, and the like are engineered and designed for their specific tasks. What supply box would be complete without a wide selection of nuts, bolts, machine screws, washers, and lock washers?

There's one other use for this book you won't want to overlook. Come holiday season, birthday, or anniversary, leave this book out in a conspicuous place and make sure it's open to the right page. It's a hint as subtle as a sledgehammer—and just as effective.

CONSTRUCTION

Benchtop Table Saw..............13

Brick Trowel.....................15

Carpenter's Square............17

Chalk Line......................19

Circular Saw....................21

Claw Hammer.....................23

Combination Square.............25

Concrete-Finishing
Trowel..........................27

Concrete Float..................29

Cordless Drill..................31

Drywall Knife...................33

Drywall Saw.....................35

Drywall Square..................37

Earmuffs........................39

Extension Cord..................41

Extension Ladder................43

Flashlight......................45

Gooseneck Bar...................47

Hole Saw........................49

Impact Driver...................51

Jigsaw..........................53

Laser Level.....................55

Level...........................57

Mason's Chisel..................59

Nail Apron/Tool Bag............61

Plumb Bob.......................63

Reciprocating Saw...............65

Safety Glasses..................67

Saw Horses......................69

Shop Vacuum.....................71

Sledgehammer....................73

Snips...........................75

Speed Square....................77

Stepladder......................79

Tape Measure....................81

Utility Knife...................83

BENCHTOP TABLE SAW

At the heart of woodworking is geometry, and geometry is filled with all kinds of shapes. In the case of furniture, we're usually talking rectangles. And nothing makes rectangles like a table saw. It's fast, it's efficient, and if you follow the manufacturer's instructions and use a push stick, it's also perfectly safe.

A benchtop table saw consists of a metal table through which a 10-inch diameter blade projects. The motor, the blade, and the geared apparatus that raises and lowers the blade and makes it tilt is housed in a cabinet below the table. You can raise or lower the blade depending on the thickness of the wood you want to cut. Today's 10-inch saws allow you to cut a piece up to 3 inches thick. Benchtop table saws make standard rip cuts and crosscuts out of the box, and once you have your saw accurately adjusted, you can use it to cut precise woodworking joints.

SHOP NOTES

PROVIDE STEADY LUBRICATION FOR BIG CUTTING JOBS
If you're doing cutting that needs constant lubrication, like using a saw to cut through concrete, a five-gallon paint bucket is a handy tool. Gouge a hole in it near the bottom [about the diameter of a screwdriver will work], and fill it with water. If someone holds it above the cut, water will leak out at just the right rate to keep the saw blade wet.

BRICK TROWEL

n the hands of a skilled mason, a brick trowel is an amazing tool. It dispenses mortar into a joint to bond bricks together, taps bricks into position, and shaves off excess mortar for a clean joint. The diamond-shaped blade of the trowel is made of high-carbon steel, with an offset tang that connects the blade and handle. The best trowels are forged blade and tang from a single piece of steel, giving them a springiness that eases the burden of working with mortar.

To use a trowel, cut into the mortar as if you were serving it up like a slice of pie. When you tip the trowel sideways, the mortar sticks slightly, allowing you to shave off the mortar onto a brick in a slicing-sweeping motion. Brick trowels come in two basic shapes: London and Philadelphia. From above, the London pattern looks like the tip of a spear. The Philadelphia pattern is broader and holds a bit more mortar. Both are good. Choose the one that feels right for you.

TIP!

USE THE BUTT END OF A BRICK TROWEL TO GENTLY BUMP A BRICK INTO PLACE
It's not unusual to place a brick in its mortar bed and find that you can't shove it completely into position, which should be about $1/16$ to $1/8$ inch back from the mason's line and level across its width and length. If you're an amateur bricklayer, you'll find that brick trowels with a bumper on the end of the handle are particularly useful. It may take a lot of bumping to nudge bricks into position.

CARPENTER'S SQUARE

A carpenter's square, also called a steel square or framing square, has been helping builders for the better part of forever. An L-shaped wonder, this tool is terrific for laying out rafters and stairs. There are two parts to this tool. The 2-inch-wide, 24-inch-long segment is the body of the square and where you'll find the rafter tables and ruler etched in. The thinner and shorter section is called the tongue. The tongue measures 16 inches from the heel to the tip and is used to mark the plumb, or vertical, for example, cuts on rafters.

Stair buttons, sold separately, are hexagonal brass buttons which are clamped onto the square's body and tongue at exact points to ensure consistency when marking stair stringers or when laying out rafters. These brass buttons act as stops for the square, so your layout is as accurate as possible.

When buying a carpenter's square, you've got a choice between aluminum and steel. Either one works fine. Don't buy chrome; a matte or painted finish will be easier to read in bright light. Having the increments etched into the blade is the best choice since this tool gets slid, flipped, and used on a number of surfaces—you don't want them to wear off. While this is a pretty tough square, it isn't impervious to damage. A good drop will knock it out of shape, as will twisting it. Handle it like the precision instrument it is designed to be.

CHALK LINE

As technology goes, the chalk line is quite simple: it's a cranked spool of string that runs through a reservoir of powdered chalk. But nothing fancy works better for marking a straight line when ripping long boards, cutting drywall, or laying out the position of wall plates while framing.

If you don't have a helper to hold the other end of the chalk line for you and the hook end won't hold, just make a notch in the wood or drywall with a razor knife, then cinch the line into the cut. Then it's just a matter of pulling the string tight like a bow string and letting go.

Not all chalk is the same. The reliable standard is blue chalk, since it is easy to see and to remove. Red chalk is nearly permanent and can stand up to some weathering, but for truly permanent marking, use dark blue, crimson, or black. If you're working with fresh concrete and don't want it to get stained, skip the colors and stick to white chalk as long as the concrete is dark enough that you'll get some contrast. For interior work like aligning wallpaper or trim details, white chalk is preferable, as it's easiest to remove and won't bleed through your work.

When the time comes to remove your mark, don't wipe it; you'll smear it into the work. Instead, blow on the chalk. And don't mix colors in the reservoir. If you need to switch colors, you're better off buying another chalk line.

WISH LIST

IRWIN MACH 6

Anybody who has reeled in an old-school chalk line could appreciate this high-speed model from IRWIN. Called the Mach6, it has a 6-to-1 metal gear assembly. For every turn of the handle, the drive gear spins six times. The line returns so rapidly, you've got to be careful to not whip yourself. You'll also appreciate its impact-resistant aluminum body, wide double-prong hook, metal crank handle, and nicely designed chalk compartment for easy access.

CIRCULAR SAW

With amperage ratings between 13 and 15 amps and armed with a 7¼-inch blade, these saws can cut nearly anything. Lock in a masonry blade and these saws will scream through concrete (this kicks up a ton of fine dust, so wear a respirator). With the right blades, you can knock through composite materials, plywood, and dimensional lumber in no time flat.

Aside from the importance of amperage (which correlates directly to the saw's power) and weight (which correlates directly to user fatigue), you want your saw to be a real fit for you. Before buying one, hold the saw and get a sense of it. Make sure it will fit your gloved hand. Other things you'll want to check are blade depth and bevel adjustments. You'll want easy-to-read adjustment scales and easy-to-reach levers.

Circular saws span a great range of models. The most popular is the side-winder circular saw, which features good durability, is light weight, and is easy to use. Need more torque and toughness? Try a worm-drive circular saw. If maneuverability for cutting sheet goods, siding, and flooring is paramount, we suggest the light 4½-inch bladed trim saw.

A fourth model is a track saw, which is the saw of choice for many scrupulous cabinetmakers and finish carpenters. These saws come with a proprietary track system, allowing you to make rips and cuts with the accuracy of a table saw, but with one advantage: portability and ease. It's far easier to push a 12-pound saw through a 95-pound sheet of medium-density fiberboard than it is to balance and push that same sheet across a table saw. If space is an issue, or just the bulk and weight of a table saw has you stalemated, a track saw is a great alternative.

CLAW HAMMER

In 30,000 BC, someone altered the destiny of the human race by lashing a stick to a rock, a refinement that increased the user's strike speed and accuracy. The hammer was born. Later, stone begat bronze, begat iron, begat steel—a material that could be forged into a ruthlessly efficient shape. Yet, after all these millennia, the wood handle remains, preferred by craftsmen for its light weight, shock absorbency, and balance. It was the post–World War II housing boom that finally transformed the profile of the modern hammer. Can't-frame-'em-fast-enough carpenters on the West Coast needed still more speed, so they grafted elements of heavy rigging hatchets onto claw hammers. The result is the beefy, all-business, California-style framer, a swift, long-handled striking tool with a vicious claw.

Hammering is a repetitive act and lots of guys have suffered from carpenter's elbow (like tennis elbow outside the country club). How do you avoid that? Get a titanium hammer from Stiletto Tools. A titanium hammer is lighter than your steel-headed counterpart and offers a significant reduction in recoil and vibration while delivering more swing force where it's really needed: hitting the nail on the head. The design improvements on the tool include a magnetic nail starting slot, a side nail puller, and a rubberized titanium handle. They still make wooden-handled hammers with titanium heads, but these newer handles are slightly curved and specifically engineered to improve your striking force with a lot less effort. Titanium hammers are expensive, but once you heft one, it'll be tough to put it back.

SHOP NOTES

HOW TO MAKE AN IMPROVISED RUBBER MALLET
For work that requires softer or non-marking impacts, a typical claw hammer can be transformed into a makeshift rubber mallet with a tennis ball. Use a utility knife to cut an X in the tennis ball, then slip it over the head of the hammer.

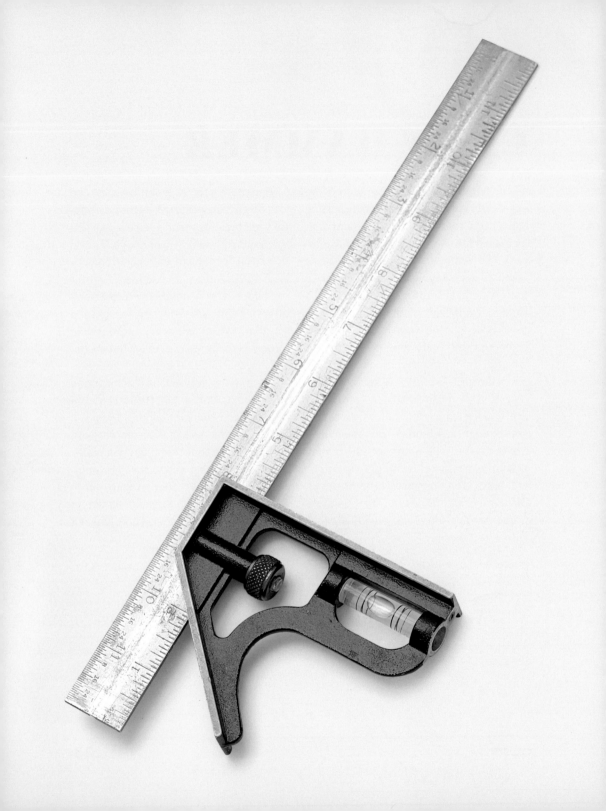

COMBINATION SQUARE

Used for marking out, measuring, and testing the squareness of corners, this versatile and useful tool was invented by Laroy Starrett in 1877. Even today, the Starrett combination square is the Rolls-Royce of these tools.

While the 12-inch blade (the ruler portion) is the most common size, many manufacturers produce other options. Squares can have blades as small as 4 inches and as long as 24 inches.

We suggest looking for a matte finish on the ruler. While chrome looks great in a display case, it won't under strong shop lights or when the sun is shining brightly. Look for a forged-steel head or cast-iron head rather than a plastic one. The forged steel is going to be more expensive, but it will be less brittle.

One of our favorites is the Starrett Combination Set (435 Series). This is not a budget tool, but this is also not a place to try to save money. The 435 Series is a versatile three-in-one with a 12-inch combination square that comes with a centering head and a reversible, adjustable protractor head. And its head is made out of durable cast iron to boot.

It's easy to use. For maximum precision, first position your pencil (or the scratch awl stored in the head), then gently slide the square to the pencil (or awl) and strike your line. Check the tool's accuracy by marking a line 90 degrees to a straightedge. Flip the square and make another mark next to the first. If the two lines are not parallel, the square is off by half the discrepancy. We suggest that you buy the best instrument you can afford and set it aside for demanding precision work.

CONCRETE-FINISHING TROWEL

You know when you see a concrete slab that wasn't well finished. The surface undulates and is coarse. It's crude. And it was probably not made with a concrete trowel. This long, thin, rectangular piece of steel has a crank-like handle mounted above it. The beauty of this trowel's design is that it allows you to move over the surface of moist concrete in a sweeping motion, leaving a smoothly finished surface in your wake.

Concrete-finishing trowels come in varying lengths, from 12 to 24 inches. The longer the trowel, the more mastery it takes to use it properly but the straighter and flatter the concrete surface you'll be able to produce.

SHOP NOTES

HOW TO MAKE YOUR OWN WORKSITE GARBAGE CAN

On the site of many big indoor jobs like, say, a home renovation, you can find a dumpster stationed outside. But there isn't always a good distribution of garbage cans near the work itself. Try this handy substitute: Since floor protection almost always arrives first, cut a sheet of the heavy cardboard [six feet usually does the trick], roll it into a cylinder, and use a spring clamp to both hold it in shape and hold open a contractor bag, creating a great on-the-spot refuse container.

CONCRETE FLOAT

Those are two words you don't see together every day. They seem mutually exclusive. But the fact is a concrete float is a necessary tool if you want to make a slab with a neat and flat surface. The concrete float consists of a handle attached to a hardwood board, a plastic slab, or a piece of magnesium. It's moved over concrete in a sweeping motion, followed by a pass with a concrete finishing trowel to really make it neat. Unlike the finishing trowel, however, you have to put some muscle into using a concrete float, pushing gravel into the wet concrete, then flattening out and pushing down large bulges and bumps. When working on exterior concrete, sometimes you stop the finishing process after using the float. Known as a float finish, this provides an anti-slip surface. For even more texture, drag a coarse broom over the floated concrete as the last step.

Like concrete trowels, floats come in varying lengths from 12 to 24 inches. The longer the float, the flatter the surface it will produce—and the more skill and effort it requires to use. That's why you'll never see a mason with weak forearms.

☆ **WISH LIST**

MARSHALLTOWN "THE HOG" MAGNESIUM FLOAT
The Marshalltown magnesium concrete float, aka The Hog, has a broad comfortable handle with an opening big enough to fit a gloved hand. And it's got a silky smooth surface and just the right balance. It's like a magic wand for concrete.

CORDLESS DRILL

Cordless drills (commonly referred to as drill/drivers) readily combine speed, power, and portability. So for most of us, they've already replaced the corded variety. Some also come with a clutch that disconnects the drive mechanism when it reaches a dialed-in force setting, preventing the user from stripping the screw.

The lithium-ion batteries of today's models allow these tools to be light, while still being workhorses. Although the 14- to 18-volt models can handle most jobs, some drills have voltages in the mid-twenties or even thirties for power that rivals that of the corded product.

If you'll be working on plumbing and running wire, a right-angle drill will make your life easier. You won't have to squeeze the drill and the bit between studs or joist bays any longer. A right-angle drill has a compact head and slim body for easy working in tight areas. Cabinetmakers might find this their drill of choice, since it's ideal for getting into tight spaces.

The keyless chuck is nice for quick bit changing, and the adjustable clutch means we can control the drill's torque. Many models are equipped with small lights. They might seem gimmicky, but they'll come in handy. Often.

Many cordless drills have a hammer drill function, which is necessary when you've got to get through concrete or dense plaster. You'd be hard-pressed to find people who don't drive screws or other fasteners with this tool. But when driving screws, change over from a Phillips-head screw to either a square drive (Robertson) or a Torx screw. You'll be happy you did.

DRYWALL KNIFE

This isn't a knife in the normal sense. Rather, it's a thin high-carbon steel blade on a handle that embeds drywall tape into a seam and then spreads an exceedingly thin layer of drywall compound over the tape. The knife is quite flexible. In fact, its springiness (combined with its smooth, straight edge) helps it leave a glass-like smooth surface in its wake. If it was too stiff, you wouldn't get a sense of how much pressure to apply.

Drywall knives are used in combination with each other. A typical patch job begins with a 4-inch or 6-inch knife to push the tape into the drywall compound and strike off any excess. The next layer of compound is applied with an 8-inch knife, then a 10-inch or 12-inch. The result is a drywall seam covered in progressively wider layers of compound that form a very shallow mound—so shallow that it blends into its surroundings. The same holds for spreading compound over interior and exterior corners and screw cavities.

ASK ROY

(Q) The crack in the hallway comes back no matter how many times I patch it. What's the right fix?

(A) Seasonal cracks in drywall and plaster are tough to repair. As they open and close, the surface around the crack crushes and grinds the patch material, or it pulls it apart. You need a super-flexible material that can bridge a wide gap, such as DAP ElastoPatch. It's about the consistency of yogurt and should be applied with a 6-inch joint-taping knife. It'll take you a few tries before you can produce a smooth finish, so experiment on an old piece of drywall first. Before you patch, use a painter's 5-in-1 tool to rake out any old repair materials. Scoop out the patch and spread it on in thin layers. Wipe off any excess [you won't be able to sand it down like joint compound], let the patch dry, then paint.

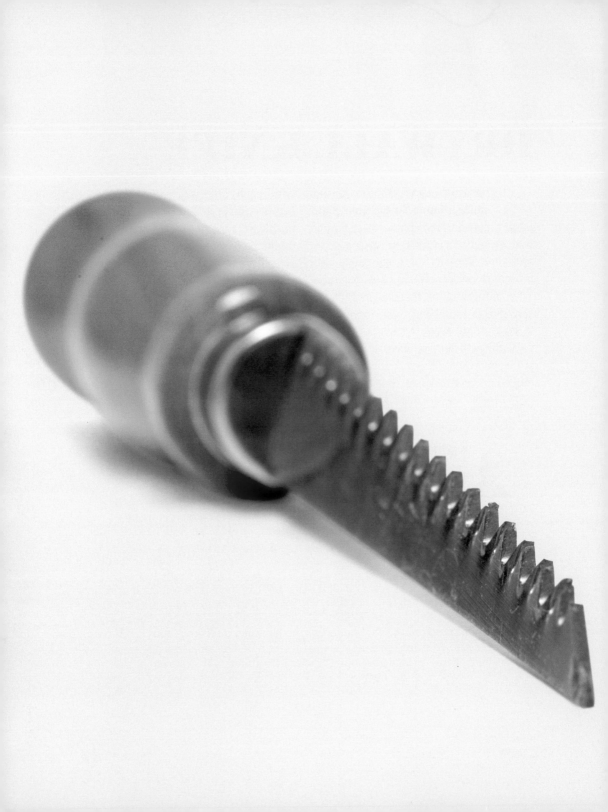

DRYWALL SAW

A drywall saw, or jab saw, is used for cutting holes for outlets and switches or, when used carefully, making a reasonably accurate hole for a recessed light. These dagger-like handsaws offer the perfect approach. After precisely transferring your measurements onto your drywall (to make the circles for recessed lights, use a compass like the one you had as a kid), push the tip of this saw through the drywall. Some tips are pretty dull but can be ground to a sharper point so that jabbing them through the drywall will be relatively clean.

The aggressive tooth is designed to cut on both the push and pull strokes. The handles are either wood, plastic, or rubberized. They all work, but if you plan on using this saw day in and day out, you might opt for a more cushioned rubberized handle. When cutting drywall where you have access to both sides of its surface, stay to the good side of the sheet, or the side that will face into the room. When you cut, it's a good idea to back cut the opening, or cut on an angle so the back of the cut is a bit wider than the front. This gives you a little "extra" room without affecting the face of the drywall.

Not all jab saws are created equal. Many manufacturers make saws that are great on standard drywall but simply will not cut cement board or dense fire-rated drywall. Search out specific makes that the manufacturers rate for these materials.

48" DRYWALL T-SQUARE 1/8"
WAL-BOARD TOOLS
FIRST IN DRYWALL TOOLS
COMP. NO 88-012
CAT. NO. WTS-50
Wallboard Tool Co., Inc
Long Beach, CA USA
MADE IN USA

DRYWALL SQUARE

You know the T square—a big drawing tool, shaped, as its name implies, like a T. Its long blade helps you draw long, straight lines that are perpendicular to an edge. Now picture that same concept but made large enough to work on a sheet of drywall.

The blade of the drywall square has inch measurements marked on it to facilitate quick and accurate cutting. There's no need to get your tape measure out. You can easily slide a utility knife along the blade to make nice clean score marks in the drywall. Score, snap, repeat. Done.

Since the blade is 48 inches long, you can crosscut a sheet of drywall in a single pass. But it gets better. The same attributes that help you quickly and neatly cut a sheet of drywall work just as well when it comes to marking plywood. If you think you can do without a drywall square, think again. It's a great tool for both drywall work and carpentry.

SHOP NOTES

HOW TO START A NAIL ONE-HANDED

For all those times you've found yourself flying solo on what should be a two-man job, here's how to start a nail with only one hand: Cup your hand over the top of the hammer, so your palm is against one side of the head. Use your fingers to hold the nail against the other side. [The nail should be perpendicular to the hammer's handle.] Now place the tip of the nail where it ought to go, then push. Lean into it a little, if it's safe [i.e., you're not atop a ladder]. With the larger surface of the hammer's head to bear on, you should be able to get the nail started just enough that it will stay in place while you begin hammering in earnest.

EARMUFFS

Hearing damage is permanent, but, fortunately, it's also preventable. Earmuffs, as opposed to earplugs or headphones, provide maximum protection. Really loud shop tools, such as chain saws and circular saws, operate above 100 decibels—and noise higher than 85 decibels begins to cause damage. OSHA (the Occupational Safety and Health Administration) requires employers to provide hearing protection if the environment noise level exceeds 85 decibels, for example.

Choose a product that has a high noise-reduction rating (NRR)—preferably in the range of 23 to 33. While earmuffs do provide optimum protection, they have to form a soundproof seal around your ears. So wearing safety glasses or having long hair will impinge on their noise-reduction ratings. Most NRRs refer to optimal conditions, so your actual noise reduction will be somewhat less than what the product is capable of achieving in a laboratory test setting.

Earplugs are not as good at sound reduction, but they aren't compromised by glasses or your choice of haircut. If optimal eye and ear protection are a must, look to the setup used by many arborists for all-around safety: a headband equipped with earmuffs that also supports a full face shield and a hard hat.

TIP!

ALWAYS PROTECT YOUR EARS
According to NIOSH [the National Institute for Occupational Safety and Health] and the CDC [Centers for Disease Control and Prevention], a continuous noise at 100 decibels can begin to cause damage in 15 minutes. And that exposure time is halved for every three decibels it increases—which means at 115 decibels, damage can occur in less than a minute.

EXTENSION CORD

Most people buy an extension cord based on length, but there are other things to consider. Extension cords are rated for indoor or outdoor use. The jacket, or insulation, on the outdoor-rated version is made to withstand temperature fluctuations, moisture, and UV radiation. Indoor cords aren't so hardy. Left exposed, an indoor-rated cord's insulating jacket will deteriorate, raising the risk of life-threatening shocks or fire.

Extension cords carry an amperage rating based on the wire's gauge and length. A wire's gauge measures the wire's diameter and determines how much current it can carry. The lower the gauge number, the larger the cable's diameter and the more current it can carry.

The amperage rating tells you how much current you can draw with a specific cord. If you plan on using a number of tools at one time, it's important to know how many amps you're going to be pulling. Amperage information is provided by Underwriters Laboratories and is printed on your tool. A 10-gauge, 100-foot power cord is a heavy hitter and should be your choice if you are using high-amperage tools farther than 50 feet from your power source. For a 50-footer, look for a 12-gauge, 15-amp cord. For most jobs 25 feet from the power outlet, a 14-gauge cord with a 15-amp rating should do the job.

TIP!

GET THE BIGGER CORD
While the extension cord's amp rating should match up to your tools, we suggest going up one wire-gauge size when in doubt. It's best to use a cord with a little extra amp capacity [also known as ampacity].

EXTENSION LADDER

anging in length from 16 to 40 feet in 2-foot increments, extension ladders put most projects safely within reach. To ensure you don't buy a ladder that comes up short, the rule of thumb is to purchase one at least 7 feet taller than the height of the object you need to reach.

When using a ladder to get on a roof, you must extend the ladder 3 feet higher than the roof, which would be three full rungs. A fully extended 24-foot ladder leaning against a house, minus the 3-foot overlap, should be 21 feet high, and the foot of the ladder should be planted 5½ feet from the wall, at a 75-degree angle.

Be aware of electrical lines; even fiberglass ladders conduct electricity. When moving your ladder into position, plan your route beforehand. To lift, squat slightly and, with your dominant hand, grab a lower rung, then reach up and grab a rung with your other hand to steady the ladder. Watch the lower part of the ladder as you walk; it will tell you if you're tilting and let you keep an eye on where you're walking.

Clearly marked on every ladder sold today are their weight limits. When you're climbing a ladder is no time to flatter yourself on your weight. And when you're on top, don't reach out to the side. If your belt buckle extends past the ladder rail, you're overreaching. When working with tools, OSHA recommends using a hand line attached to a bucket and that you pull your tools up once you are in a safe working position.

TIP!

TRY THE COMBINATION LADDER
Do you need both a stepladder and an extension ladder? Consider Werner's Telescoping Multi-Position Ladder. It converts into a scaffold as well, and features configurations for stairwells.

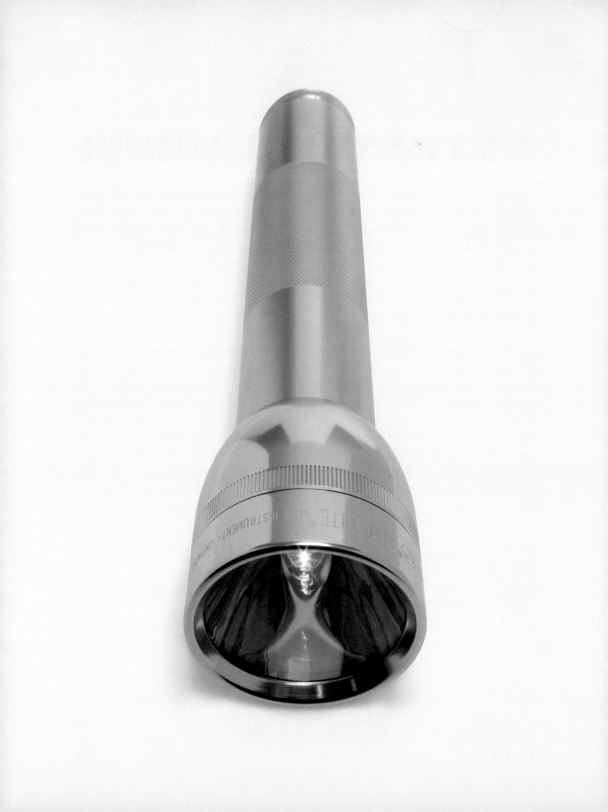

FLASHLIGHT

Working one-handed with a flashlight, or worse yet, with a light clamped between your teeth, is no way to operate. A camping headlamp is useful, since it holds the light for you and always aims where you're looking, or there's a variety of stationary lights with magnetic handles or movable necks that help, too.

We buy flashlights for one reason, and that's to illuminate a dark space. So lumens, a measure of brightness, matter. The more lumens a flashlight boasts, the brighter and farther the light will shine. Some manufacturers still rate brightness in candlepower; one candlepower is equal to 12.57 lumens.

Bulb type matters in both longevity of the bulb and batteries. Incandescent and xenon lights are battery eaters, since they use battery power to create heat and light, though xenon lights do provide very bright light. LEDs, or light-emitting diodes, last longest of the bulbs and are easiest on the batteries, but the quality of light isn't as good as xenon bulbs. Some LEDs produce clean white light, but many are tinted.

Casing material may be important, depending on the type of work you're doing. If camping, fishing, or plumbing is in your future, then a rugged aluminum body and water-resistant casing are certainly some things to consider. But if it's a just-in-case type of light to get you around during a power failure or the light you reach for in the middle of the night after hearing a mysterious creak come from downstairs in the kitchen, then a plastic body will do just fine.

SHOP NOTES

HOW TO BUILD A BASIC WORK LIGHT
```
Coil a few loops of 12-gauge copper wire around
a flashlight's barrel and twist the rest into a
base. Aim as needed.
```

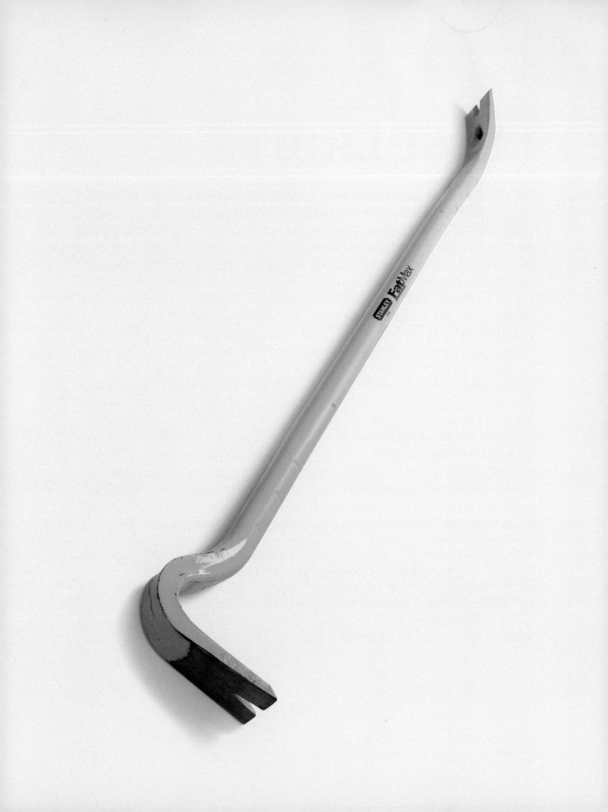

GOOSENECK BAR

This is also called a wrecking bar—for good reason. A curved neck gives this steel tool incredible prying power, perfect for separating two pieces of lumber that are nailed together. Rely on small models up to 18 inches long for light-duty demolition, and keep a 36-inch bar on hand for the really big stuff.

The gooseneck bar is a dual-headed tool. The chisel end is great for lifting heavy stones when landscaping and for prying things apart, like frozen firewood. The gooseneck end usually has a split claw that's great for driving under the head of a nail that you need to remove. The curved neck provides a tremendous amount of leverage in a small amount of space.

You've probably seen these bars featured on any number of home improvement television shows. What they show is the more entertaining aspect of this tool, when it's used as a striking instrument. For breaking up tile, cabinets, studs, or just about anything in your way, the impact from this lever is focused on a small striking point, usually the gooseneck bend, creating an enormous amount of force. Wearing safety goggles is a must when using this tool, as is a warning cry to let other people in the area know that there may be flying debris. "Fire in the hole!" is a fun option.

TIP!

USE THE BAR CORRECTLY
Use the pry bar end [near the curve] to pull out nails sticking ¼ inch or more out of a piece of wood. If that doesn't do it, some wrecking bars have a teardrop notch in the flat end, which is useful to get additional pull where necessary—a humongous help.

HOLE SAW

There's a great way to make a large hole quickly and neatly, and that is by using a hole saw. As its name implies, it's a round-bodied saw that's chucked onto a drill, and it cuts a hole through wood, drywall, and ceiling tiles. (There are also specialized metal-cutting hole saws that electricians and metal fabricators use.) Rather than producing wood chips like a drill bit or an auger bit, the hole saw produces a cylindrical piece of waste wood. You need to remove this block of waste wood from the saw, and that's why there's a diagonal slot in their side wall or a hole in the bottom. You stick a screwdriver into the slot, dig in behind the piece of waste

wood, and pry it out. And then it's on to the next hole.

Basic woodcutting hole saws come in two types. Less expensive models are made from plain carbon steel. These give good service for most soft building materials, such as wood and drywall. However, manufacturers also make hole saws with bimetal construction. The tooth is a tough, long-wearing tool steel or even carbide, and the saw body is plain carbon steel or spring steel. The tooth is brazed onto the saw body, and the result is such a tough saw that it will cut wood and even light-gauge steel or soft metals, such as aluminum and brass.

★ **WISH LIST**

LENOX BI-METAL HOLE SAW
Hole saws lead a tough life. The Lenox Bi-metal saw is the toughest of the tough with a thick body and sharp, rugged teeth that withstand wood, metal, and abrasive plastics. But they're easy on you. Their unique design allows you to pop a hole saw off its arbor in seconds and switch to another size. And you do that without tools.

IMPACT DRIVER

If you're still using a drill/driver to drive screws, you don't know what you're missing. An impact driver operates with about 1,400 inch-pounds of torque—triple what a drill puts out—without delivering that torque to the handle of the tool like a cordless drill would. That alone saves your wrist from some serious next-day aching.

Impact drivers are designed to do one thing well, and that's drive screws. Drill/drivers, on the other hand, are effective screwdrivers, but their effectiveness drops off with larger fasteners, especially really big ones, like lag screws. Impact drivers combine rotation with concussive blows to improve their screwdriving capability, especially when sinking a fastener in tough material, like pressure-treated lumber.

Right now, lithium-ion-powered tools are the best option. They are much lighter, and the batteries charge faster and hold their charge longer than NiCad or NiMH batteries do. As with a cordless drill, be sure to buy an impact driver that comes with a light. When you're in a dark attic putting in some duct work or working under a deck, it's a blessing. The other thing you'll want, aside from a belt hook, is a place to stow extra bits on the tool.

With all this extra power, make sure your drill bits and socket adapters are strong enough to handle it. Most impact drivers have a ¼-inch hex-shaped chuck. That's a lot of torque being applied to a thin-shanked bit or driver. Impact-rated driver bits and sockets are easy enough to find at home centers and online, and they last much longer than the standard sockets or bits.

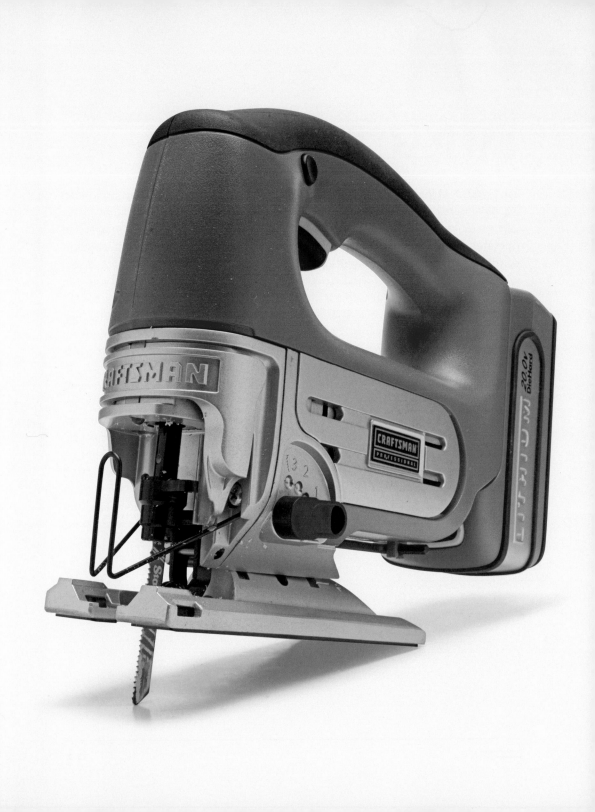

JIGSAW

The real bread-and-butter use for a jigsaw is cutting freehand curves in wood, metal, or plastic. Achieving these graceful curves, semicircles, or arcs take some practice. While we advise cutting wide of your line and then sanding, filing, or planing your material into its final shape, having the right blade makes a big difference. Thin blades with a higher tpi (teeth per inch) are the most maneuverable and cleanest-cutting. A thick blade with fewer teeth is for roughing a shape close to where you want it.

Cutting freehand circles with a jigsaw is tough to get right, but using a trammel is an excellent way to cut spot-on curves and circles. For smaller circles, though, nothing beats a good hole saw on your cordless drill.

There's more this saw can do. Another cool function is coping crown molding. The Collins coping foot is an aftermarket base that fits most jigsaws and turns them into power coping saws. Like any other skill, coping takes some practice to get just right.

Not every saw performs equally, so before purchasing this tool, make sure to consider the features available, which include hands-free blade changing, blade guides (to keep the blade cutting square to the base), and splinter guards to minimize tear-out. (Tear-out is nothing more than a splintery cut made in wood.)

STEER THE SAW FOR STRAIGHTER CUTS

TIP! Freehand cuts with a jigsaw are nearly impossible. Instead, steer the saw along a clamped-down straightedge guide, such as a steel square or long level. As you feed the blade into the cut, place one hand on the edge of the saw's baseplate, and press in toward the straightedge. Advance the saw slowly with even pressure. For more precise steering, clamp down a second, parallel to the first and separated by the width of the saw's baseplate plus $1/16$ of an inch. Make the cut by steering the saw between the two straightedges.

LASER LEVEL

Years ago carpenters went through great effort to mark a level line on the outside or inside of a building before working on a project. They used levels, strings, and their own well-developed eyes. Things are a lot easier today, thanks to the laser level. The device consists of a rotating laser generator or a stationary line generator that projects a red or green line around the circumference of a room or even just against one wall. To position it at the right height, laser levels can be attached to a specialized pole that spans the floor and ceiling. Or, if you don't have one of those, you can always just set the level on something that is about the right height, such as a sawhorse. Simple lasers project a single line, but many today project multiple lines, perpendicular to each other. For example, one line may run up the wall vertically and over the ceiling, while another line marks the wall horizontally.

The laser level can do a number of things for you. It may form a level line for installing something like a chair rail. Or it may mark the bottom line of kitchen cabinets. Suppose you're working in an old house where walls, ceilings, and floors are all out of whack. You can use the laser level to establish what's known as a datum—a reliable reference or starting point from which you can make accurate measurements and installation. It's the old "you gotta start somewhere." And that somewhere is with a laser level.

WISH LIST

BOSCH GCL 2-160

With a working range of 65 feet, the Bosch GCL 2-160 packs a lot of versatility and laser power into a tool about the size of a large tape measure. It's our go-to tool in the *Popular Mechanics* office for construction projects where we need speed, ease of use, and dead-on accuracy in horizontal or cross line modes. Built to IP54 standards, it's more than capable of withstanding the typical dirt and moisture that it will encounter on a construction site.

LEVEL

There's a level for every job, and there's no downside to having more than a few different varieties and sizes of this essential tool. At a minimum, your toolbox should have a 2-foot and a 9-inch torpedo level. You'll reach for the most commonly used level, the 2-foot (or even 4-foot), all the time. Not only will you use it for big projects like leveling appliances or bookshelves, because it comes with a bonus: Long levels make a nice straightedge.

For small jobs, pull out the pocket-size 9-inch torpedo level, perfect for hanging pictures or setting shelves. Many torpedo levels have a magnetized side, and the vials have markings not just for leveling but for pitching drainpipes as well. But far be it from us to limit your level collection to just these two. Here are two more types of levels we suggest:

Use a line level when building a deck, fence, or any other long spanning job. It's designed to hang on a string with two small hooks and is so light it won't bow the string.

A post level can be strapped to deck piers, columns, or flagpoles for hands-free plumbing. The 90-degree bend in the level reads plumb front to back and side to side simultaneously.

SHOP NOTES

USE SANDPAPER TO PREVENT LEVEL SLIPPAGE

When you're holding a long level against the wall to make markings for a shelf or TV mount, it's impossible to hold an end in each hand and operate the pencil. But if you hold only one end, the other has a tendency to slip, especially as you make your marking. Keep it in place by folding a piece of sandpaper in half and putting it grain-side-out between the level and the wall. Friction keeps the level still.

MASON'S CHISEL

If you work with bricks and concrete blocks, invariably some of those will need to be cut to length. Instead of using a wet saw, masons turn to the time-honored method of scoring and breaking bricks with a mason's chisel. The stout tool is formed from a block of tool steel that is shaped and hardened to withstand the demands of striking such hard and abrasive materials.

The average mason's chisel has a cutting edge slightly more than two inches wide, but it may be as wide as three inches. That width is important: It's wider than the depth of a brick.

To cut a brick, mark its length with a carpenter's pencil or score a line on its face with a brick trowel. Next, hold the brick flat on a solid surface. Place the mason's chisel on the mark and tap it with a stout hand sledgehammer or a big ball-peen hammer. Do this on both wide faces and one narrow edge to leave a deep score mark on the three faces. Turn the brick on its remaining edge and make a score mark on it as you did the other three faces. Then give the chisel a good firm hit with the hammer. The brick should break neatly along the scored line.

SHOP NOTES

A QUIRKY SUBCATEGORY: THE PLUGGING CHISEL
What It Is: a masonry chisel used to cut deteriorated mortar from between bricks. The chunk of mortar it removes is shaped like a plug, but more likely it takes its name from the slang definition of plug—to hit—but also to work hard at something, as in "to plug away at it." Removing deteriorated mortar with this tool is hard work. Try it. You'll see.

NAIL APRON/ TOOL BAG

We've all been there. We're in the middle of some kind of a project and we start sticking tools in our pockets. That's okay if all we're talking about is a screwdriver and a pair of pliers. But often you run out of pockets pretty quickly. And there hasn't been a pocket made yet that's particularly good at storing nails, sharp screws, or a hammer.

That's why you need a nail apron and tool bag. Whether it's a simple $5 nail apron with the name of a lumber yard printed on it or a beautiful leather tool bag that hangs from your shoulders with padded straps, the point is, you want to keep your pockets clear and be able to use and store the tools you need for the job while remaining mobile.

Aprons come in two types. Simple nail aprons fasten around your waist. These are made in a variety of materials from inexpensive cotton to canvas to leather. These will carry a hammer, some fasteners, and a couple of hand tools, such as a utility knife or a couple pairs of pliers. You'll probably have to augment your storage using a back pocket. Larger aprons look more like a hybrid between a chef's apron and a tool belt. A neck loop fastens the apron over your head, and a waist belt clips or ties around your midsection. The apron may reach down to your knees or only as far down as your waist.

Tool bags are another creature entirely. They fasten around your waist or hang from your shoulders with clip-on suspenders or padded shoulder straps. They'll hold anything from a nail gun to hand tools to several pounds of fasteners. These bags are made from leather or high-wear synthetic fabrics.

PLUMB BOB

There are some truly ancient tools in the kit of every carpenter: the hammer, the saw, the plane. The built environment relies on them. It also relies on the plumb bob, a cone-shaped piece of brass or steel suspended from a piece of string. Lowered down from one point to another, it uses the force of gravity to accurately mark a line in vertical space. It's as simple and ingenious as the wheel, and it's about as culturally important.

Let's take one example of importance drawn from remodeling. Suppose you make a hole in a floor and want to project that opening to the exact same spot on the floor below, for the sake of building a wall or marking the landing of a set of stairs, yet to be installed. From one corner of the opening or from any point on it, you lower the plumb down to the floor below. Carefully mark the point where the tip of the plumb bob touches the floor, and there you have it: bingo, a precise reference point extended down from above.

★ **WISH LIST**

KRAFT TOOL PROFESSIONAL BRASS PLUMB BOB

One obvious quality of a Kraft plumb bob is that it's solid brass, not brass-plated steel. But it has other qualities that the inexperienced may overlook. It has a hardened steel tip that's replaceable and at the other end, its cap is removable allowing you to get the string perfectly aligned in its center.

RECIPROCATING SAW

The reciprocating saw is one of those indispensable tools that proves its worth the first time you go to install a door or skylight or, for that matter, do nearly any demolition task around the house. It's not a precision instrument, but in the right hands, you might think it is. The saw works like an aggressive electric carving knife. The blade reciprocates at tremendous speed and power. Combine that with blade sizes ranging from a mere 3 inches to 16 inches long and there isn't anything you can't cut with one of these tools, from a rusty bolt to a piece of lumber to a stubborn tree root. The blades are designed for specific tasks. There are specific wood-cutting blades, and there are blades strictly for metal use. Additionally, bimetal blades can cut through wood, metal, and other miscellaneous materials at the same time. There are even diamond-grit blades, which excel at particularly tough jobs, like cutting cast-iron pipe.

A good reciprocating saw will have a double-insulated body to reduce the risk of shocks, even if you cut a live electrical wire. (It happens.) Many models have variable speeds, which is a necessity for this kind of tool, since it is used to cut plastic, plaster, metal, wood, asphalt shingles, tree limbs—you name it. Emergency responders, like firefighters and EMT crews, carry these saws to perform many tasks, including vehicle extrications.

Electricians, plumbers, and landscapers, who don't use the saw the way a remodeler does, might be well-served by a cordless model. But for those heavy-duty jobs, grab hold of an industrial-quality 15-amp variable-speed saw with an orbital cutting option. It'll tear through just about anything in front of it.

SAFETY GLASSES

Safety glasses are the single most important tool you'll ever own. You know the old saying, "It's all fun and games until someone loses an eye." Well, don't let anything get in the way of a good old time, then.

We're not talking about those goofy goggles we had to wear in high school that looked like a scuba diver's mask. We mean stylish glasses that could probably replace your favorite sunglasses.

Many manufacturers offer glasses with adjustable rubberized frames for maximum comfort. While comfort is important, it is recommended that the glasses provide maximum coverage and are made from high-impact plastic. But that's not all the protection you'll need, since you'll wear these indoors and out:

glare reduction is also a must. Smoke-tinted or mirrored lenses will certainly reduce the risk of sun blindness, but make sure your glasses also meet the stringent ANSI Z87.1-2003 UV protection ratings. While you're at it, get antifog lenses, too. Let nothing interrupt your view, especially when you've got a power tool with a razor-sharp bit spinning at 10,000 rpm in your hands.

Switching back and forth between prescription glasses and safety glasses can be a huge pain. The only thing worse is saddling a set of safety goggles over your prescription glasses. But you don't have to sweat it anymore. For the ultimate tool kit, invest in a pair of prescription safety glasses so you can focus on other things.

SAW HORSES

These you can actually make yourself. You'll save a few bucks—and show people you're a serious craftsperson. It was a carpenter's calling card once upon a time, and for some it still is. You should plan to spend a few hours making it, but it will be worth it.

The choice of lightweight but sturdy materials is as much a component as the execution of the compound angles or the selection of additional features, such as braces, slots, and shelves.

Using 8 x ¾–inch stock for the top, simply scribe and notch the lumber for the legs to fit. Legs are reinforced with a gusset plate that also acs as a support for the top, making them real workhorses. Whenever you make a wood-to-wood connection, remember this mantra: screws and glue always prove true.

Your saw horses can be used as a temporary work table, to hold lumber for cutting, as tool stands, and more.

TIP!

YOU CAN BUILD YOUR OWN SAW HORSES

If you're ready to get to work on crafting these versatile accessories, go to popularmechanics.com/sawhorse for detailed blueprints and step-by-step instructions on how to build a sturdy and versatile set of saw horses. The classic design provides a wide work surface and legs angled in two directions for stability. The only lumber required is a few 2 x 4s. you may actually have enough in your scrap pile, but if not, you won't have to spend more than $20. It's a project that will help you make other projects. You'll find uses for them everywhere.

SHOP VACUUM

They look like small garbage cans on wheels, and their appetite for workshop waste is nothing short of voracious. Designed to pick up debris a household vac would choke on in seconds, wet-dry vacs also inhale liquids with blinding speed and have cleanup compartments measured in gallons, and the mess goes into a water tight, washable drum instead of a bag.

Smaller machines typically have a 2- to 4-gallon capacity with motors around 3 horsepower. For most around-the-house cleanups, these machines are ideal. For home workshops or job sites, you'll want a larger machine. Midrange shop vacs will have 10- to 20-gallon capacities and 5-horsepower motors. These machines are pretty loud but can suck up just about anything that's not nailed down.

With a little ingenuity and PVC pipe, you can use a shop vac as a dust collection system in your home shop. Also, several manufacturers make models that work in conjunction with your power tools. Flip the switch to your router, sander, or saw, and the vacuum kicks in—which is great when you're working inside the house. The vacuum will shut off a few seconds after the tool, just to make sure that it's grabbed all the sawdust.

If your vacuum isn't picking up the way it used to, there's a good chance the filter is clogged. It just gets too worn, damp, or dirty to be effective. Replace it. You'll literally breathe easier. And your vacuum will work.

SHOP NOTES

ADAPT YOUR SHOP VAC TO PICK UP DROPPED VALUABLES

When you drop a tray of small parts, like short screws or plastic wire connectors, it's a nightmare to pick them up. Find a thin, porous piece of fabric like an old undershirt, tear off a small piece, and stretch it over the end of the vacuum's hose. Secure it with rubber bands. Then use the vacuum to pick up the pieces. The fabric allows air through but keeps the parts at the end of the hose.

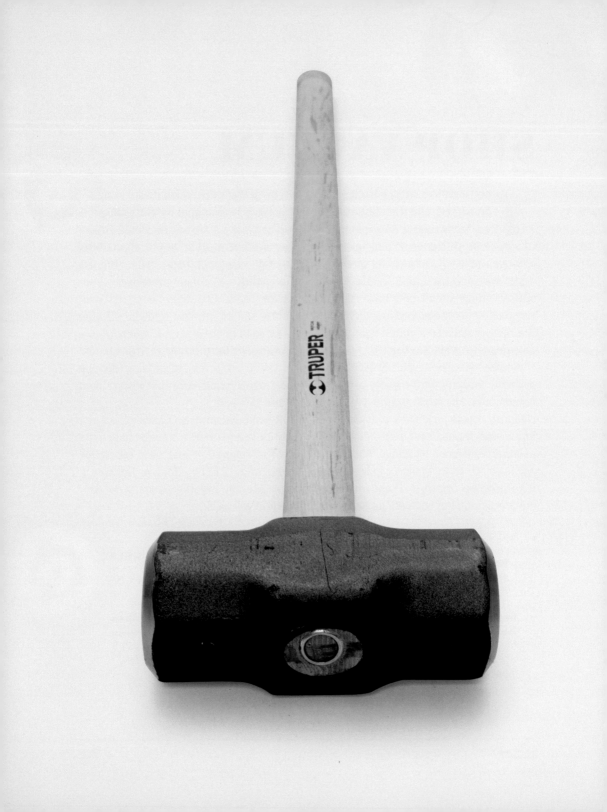

SLEDGEHAMMER

Few tools combine brute force and finesse as elegantly as a sledge-hammer. There's something therapeutic about hefting a sledge to pulverize an ugly, old brick stoop or to drive some fence posts. With a wedge and a sledge, you can split some firewood and get your own stove burning, too. Most of us are better off with an easy-to-swing 8- or 10-pound sledge with an unbreakable fiberglass handle, as opposed to a 16- to 20-pounder.

This dynamic tool isn't just used for destructive purposes. It can be used to align the legs of a door opening. Use a sacrificial block and place it against the side you need to shift. The block will protect the framing from the destructive force of the steel head and distribute it along the wall. With a controlled knock or two, you can straighten out cross-legged door openings, salvage architectural elements, or position plywood subflooring so the sheets get snugged together without damage.

Using a sledge for any length of time can be a real workout. But, if you've got some Tom Sawyer in you, you might just convince one of the younger guys how great it feels and let them take a swing at it.

SWING YOUR SLEDGEHAMMER CORRECTLY

TIP!

Swinging a sledge is 10 percent strength and 90 percent skill. Position yourself with your left foot ahead of your right [for right-handers] and just right behind your target. You'll want to arc the swing as high and tall as possible; this will let gravity provide the force behind your strike. Your right hand should begin the swing at the top of the handle, under the head, and then slide down the grip to meet your left hand near its base at the impact.

SNIPS

You don't have to be a metalworker to appreciate snips. This tool cuts steel, copper, or aluminum sheets and also cuts rubber, heavy cardboard, and plastic. Pro models have color-coded handles to indicate whether they are designed for left curves, right curves, or straight cuts (red, green, and yellow, respectively). Some blades have a serrated edge, which helps you keep a grip on the metal but leaves a more ragged cut than a nonserrated blade. Most homeowners can get by with a single all-purpose utility snip.

Your first time cutting with a pair of snips may be challenging. Snips are not scissors for metal. To make a cut, pull the bottom blade up and keep the top blade lined up with your cut line. For long cuts in sheet metal, use an awl to mark the cut line. Be careful, and use a straightedge; don't freehand it. And don't rush it.

When you work with any type of sheet metal, wear a pair of heavy-duty leather gloves. A freshly cut piece of sheet metal is very sharp.

As for a preference on the model of snips to purchase, consider offset aviation snips. The offset blades keep your hands clear of the work, and they offer a more natural cutting position while giving better leverage to cut thicker material. Also known as compound-action snips, sheet snips, or maille snips, these powerhouses were developed to cut aluminum in aircraft construction and can handle aluminum up to 18 gauge, stainless steel up to 26 gauge, and mild steel up to 24 gauge with ease.

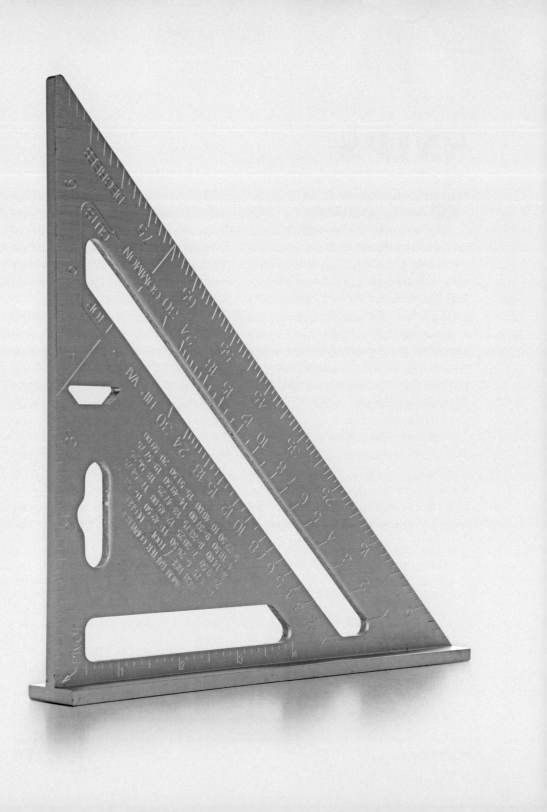

SPEED SQUARE

A lickety-split crosscutting fence for a circular saw is just one function of this terrific little tool. It's actually a rafter angle square. The name Speed Square is the registered trademark of the Swanson Tool Company. It was invented by Albert J. Swanson in 1925, and he dubbed the name Speed Square because it provides a shortcut for measurements and angle calculations. In fact, it is the preferred square for marking rafter angles, over and above the framing square.

You'll be hard-pressed to find a carpenter without an apron-handy 7-inch version of this tool. For marking crosscuts and layout lines, these tools are a breeze to use, and many have notches to help guide a pencil point, for marking a long rip in wood. This tool is terrific for quickly zeroing in a chop saw simply by checking the blade against the fence: lay the square against the back fence to make sure the blade is aligned for a 90-degree cut, then set the square on the miter saw's bed to check that the blade is perpendicular. Now your portable precision saw is ready for work. And another nice thing about this square: when you drop it—and it will happen—you can bet it will stay true thanks to the strength of a triangle. Try that with a combination square or L-shaped framing square.

These squares come in two sizes. The 7-inch is a pocketable accessory, while the 12-inch version is the go-to tool for rafter and stair layouts. And don't sweat rafter calculations. Better models come with a great reference guide on how to get the most out of this must-own tool.

STEPLADDER

The safest way to reach things inside the house is with a properly sized stepladder. Although they range in height from 3 to 20 feet, the most useful ladders are those in the 6- to 10-foot range. It should be tall enough for you to change a lightbulb but not so large as to be unwieldy. For use on stairs and uneven surfaces like driveways, ramps, or curbs, a versatile ladder like an adjustable Little Giant ladder might fit your needs.

When using a typical stepladder, you should stand at least 2 feet from the top. The maximum working height is about 3 feet above the top of the ladder. So a 5-foot stepladder will provide a safe and effective working height of 8 feet. Many ladder-related accidents are a result of falls, and these rules are provided to offer optimal balance for the user. The other danger with stepladders is when tools are left on the top of the ladder and then forgotten. When the ladder is later moved, the tools come raining down, and if it's a hammer or screwdriver, that can hurt.

One big rule is the same as with an extension ladder: Don't lean to reach. You always want that belt buckle between the ladder rails. Also, don't use a stepladder as a leaning ladder. Stepladders should only be used in a fully opened position with the side and cross braces locked. And finally, unless stated otherwise by the manufacturer, stepladders should never be used as a poor man's scaffold. Never use a stepladder to support a work platform.

TAPE MEASURE

measuring tape is a spring-loaded marvel, combining compactness, accuracy, and speed. A 25-foot model is sufficiently long to handle most home construction projects, yet small and light enough to stash in a nail pouch or clip to your jeans. But there's more to consider.

Locking devices keep the tape from rewinding. A slide lock is at the front of the tape rule; it's easy to reach and rarely unlocks unexpectedly. A lever lock performs the same function but is located on the base of the tool. A lever lock is easier to engage than a slide lock, but some people complain it's too easy to accidentally unlock when in use.

STANLEY FATMAX tape is one beefy tape. The blade is 1¼" wide and, combined with its concave shape, can be horizontally extended for 11 feet without support. This extra strength is appreciated when you are measuring for crown molding or finding the right spot to hang a ceiling fan. The tape itself is easy to read. The half, quarter, and sixteenth scales are clearly marked, and there's no metric conversion on the other side of the scale to confuse the user.

Now, you might notice that the hook end of your tape measure shifts a bit. That's supposed to happen. It's designed to move the distance of its own thickness. This ensures that inside measurements will be exactly the same as if you hooked it on the end of a board. To keep that hook from getting damaged, don't let that tape whip closed. Slow the retraction speed with your finger and you'll keep that tape a good long time.

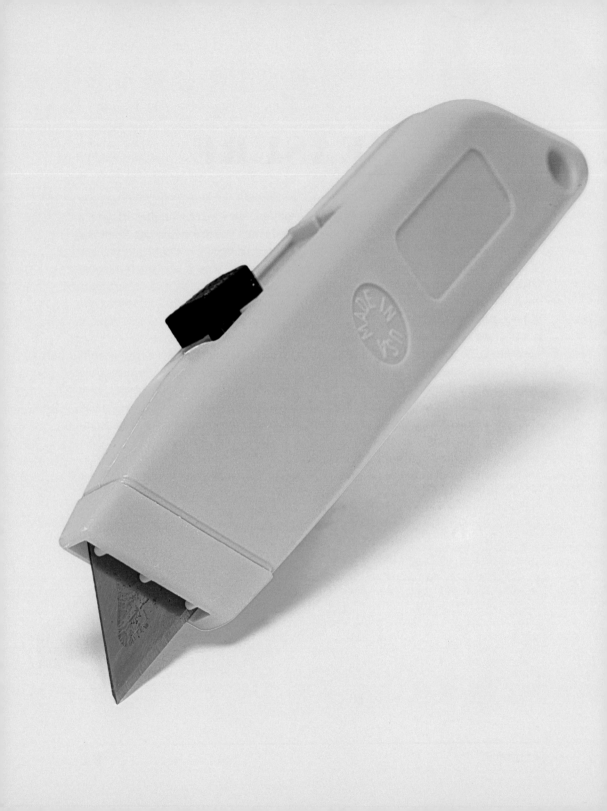

UTILITY KNIFE

Utility knives have come a long way since their introduction. With tool-free access to blade storage in the handle and smooth-sliding retractable blades, newer versions of the tool are easier to use, offer a better grip, and may include other features, such as a slot for slitting string. There are also folding versions, which work much like a pocket knife. They are easy to stow in a pocket, and many come with a belt clip.

The beauty of the utility knife lies in its simplicity. Like many great tools, it isn't designed for one particular purpose but instead is absolutely indispensable for tackling dozens of jobs. If you've been using yours only to cut twine and open packages, then you've been missing out. There's a lot this little tool can do: from cutting batts of insulation to making mincemeat of cardboard; trimming wood shims to scribing hinge mortises; opening packages to rescuing paint-coated screws.

It can even sharpen your carpenter's pencils, which comes in handy more often than you might think. You'll have to agree: It's more than just a handle with a sharp, pointy blade, right?

 TIP!

GET THE BEST
Utility knives with minimal bells and whistles won't break the bank, running between $5 and $15. Even the inexpensive ones are useful. But for a few extra bucks you can find a knife that feels comfortable in your grip and has easy-access blade storage, so you'll never have to scrounge for a replacement. Take a look at STANLEY and CRAFTSMAN for dependable models.

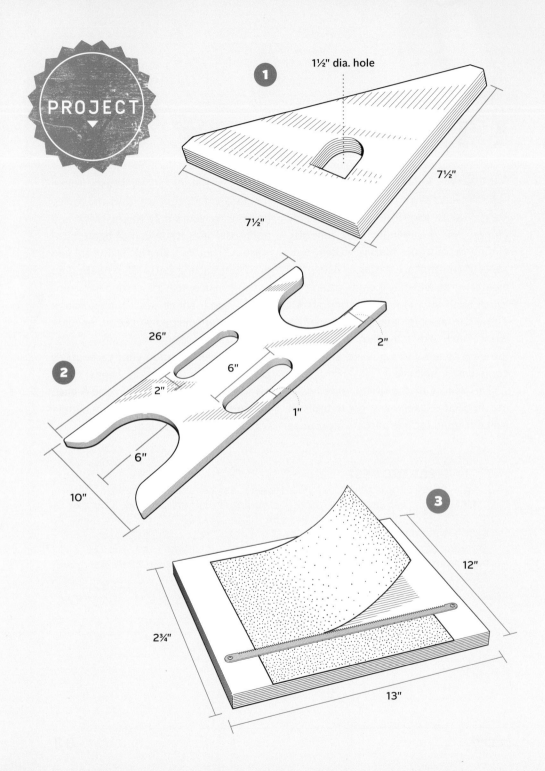

PROJECT ▼

1

1½" dia. hole

7½"

7½"

2

26"

2"

6"

2"

1"

10"

6"

3

12"

2¾"

13"

Three DIY Worksite Essentials

1 **WORK TRIANGLES**
Cut these out of scrap ¾-inch birch or AC plywood, using the factory 90-degree corner. Standard models are 6-inch and 8-inch, but make them any size you like. Cut the opening for a clamp head using a holesaw, then use a jigsaw to make a flat surface parallel to the sides. It's best not to get too attached to them. That way you can saw, drill, or screw into them as needed. When they're chewed up, toss them and make another bunch.

2 **CORD WRAPPER**
These can be cut from scrap ¾-inch plywood. This one is 10 inches wide by 26 inches long. Its handholds are 2 inches wide by about 6 inches long, set 1 inch in from each outside edge. It easily holds a 50-foot 12-gauge cord. Mark out the pattern and saw it to shape with a jigsaw. Use a belt sander to knock off any irregularities, then run counterclockwise around its perimeter with a rounding-over bit in a router. Do this on both faces to ensure nicely rounded surfaces that won't damage the cord or give you a splinter. Some guys skip the handholds while others cut a slot to tuck in both ends of the cable. Pick what's best for you.

3 **SANDPAPER RIPPER**
Everybody has a different take on this thing. One *Popular Mechanics* contributor built his with a fence and graduated settings marked on the board to suit different sanders in his shop. This one is more simple. It's built from a scrap piece of ¾-inch plywood to rip paper for an old-school rubber 3M sanding block. The design lets you hold and rip the larger piece of paper rather than the smaller piece. Or put the hacksaw teeth facing the opposite way and rip the smaller piece. Whichever way you choose, an 18-tpi hacksaw blade is about right for a clean, fast tear.

WOODWORKING

5-in-1 Tool...........................89

Awl...................................91

Bar Clamp............................93

Bench Plane..........................95

Block Plane..........................97

C Clamp..............................99

Caulk Gun...........................101

Coping Saw..........................103

Crosscut Saw........................105

Dust Mask...........................107

Fast-Action Clamp..................109

Marking Gauge.......................111

Miter Saw...........................113

Nail Set............................115

Paintbrush/Roller...................117

Pocket Hole Jig.....................119

Putty Knife.........................121

Random Orbital
Sander..............................123

Router..............................125

Sharpening Stones...................127

Shoulder Plane......................129

Spring Clamp........................131

Wood Chisel.........................133

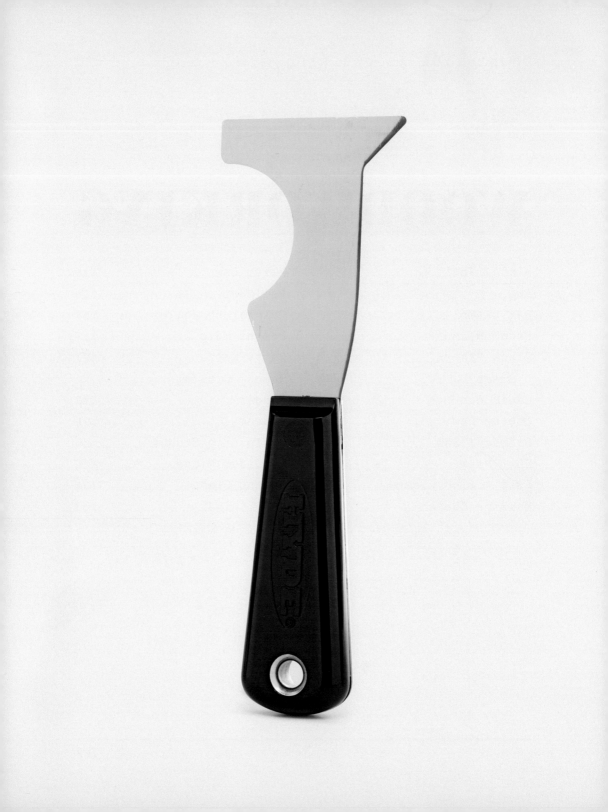

5-IN-1 TOOL

This jack-of-all-trades tool has a ⁵⁄₆₄-inch-thick blade. It's a scraper, putty knife, pick, paint roller squeegee, and can opener, and some 6-in-1 models have a metal cap on the end of the handle for bumping in loose drywall nails.

The pointy pick is great for cleaning out crevices, starting an edge to remove old caulking, pulling staples, and even cleaning off a boot sole. The forward flat edge works great as a paint scraper, and you can ease it behind a delicate piece of trim you want to remove. The short flat side is perfect for prying open a can of paint, urethane, or stain. Wrap the tool in a cloth and you can soak up a spill in the slenderest crack. The blade is stiff and wide enough for applying putty, wood filler, or joint compound to small imperfections.

Flip the tool over and you've got a tap hammer to set the paint can's lid back in place. And that little pick on the side is great at removing dried paint that would interfere with getting that lid sealed.

The polished blade makes cleaning these tools pretty easy, but best of all is the tool's portability. It slips smoothly into your back pocket. And, of course, there's the price. Budget models start at around $5, and you can find them nearly anywhere. Keep your eyes peeled for the 6-in-1. You'll use that drywall nail setter more than you think.

★ WISH LIST

HYDE 5-IN-1 MULTI-TOOL
There's a reason Hyde Tools are legends in the paint trades. You can't break them and you can wear them out only if you try really, really hard. That's because their blades are made from tough high-carbon steel and their handle attaches to that blade with rivets. For scraping, cutting, spreading, paint roller cleaning and a host of other jobs that painter's do, the black-and-silver Hyde tool has withstood the test of time. And then some.

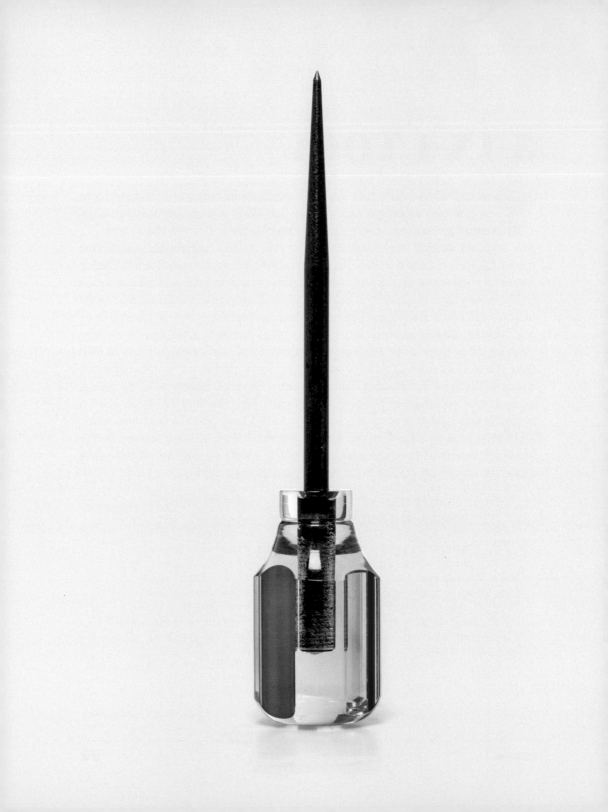

AWL

A single measuring tape indicates the length of everything from lumber to copper, but when it comes time to mark those measurements, the tool to use depends on the material. Keeping the line clear and legible is one of the keys to an accurate cut. Keep an awl in your toolbox and you'll be ready for any surface when you need to make your mark.

The most common of these tools is a scratch awl. A scratch awl is a layout tool used for marking when a pencil or marker either leaves a line that's too thick or won't leave a mark at all on the chosen workpiece. Honed to a fine point, a scratch awl is an extremely precise marking tool reserved for when craftsmen are working with tight tolerances. To use one, place a straightedge next to the awl where you need to make your mark. Angle the awl so the point is against the straightedge, then pull the scratch awl toward you along the straightedge. One thing about using an awl is that once you've made your cut line, you can't erase it. An awl's point is less likely to wander than a knife blade's if you are marking hardwoods, sheet metal, or leather, and it's a staple in many shops.

There are two basic varieties: awls with a slender shaft and a delicate tip, and the more robust models, with a broad tip and a shank like a screwdriver. The first is used by woodworkers and metalworkers to scribe a sharp line; the other is used by electricians and other tradesmen to mark lines, poke holes, and scratch off rust and dirt. Depending on your needs, stock just one or both.

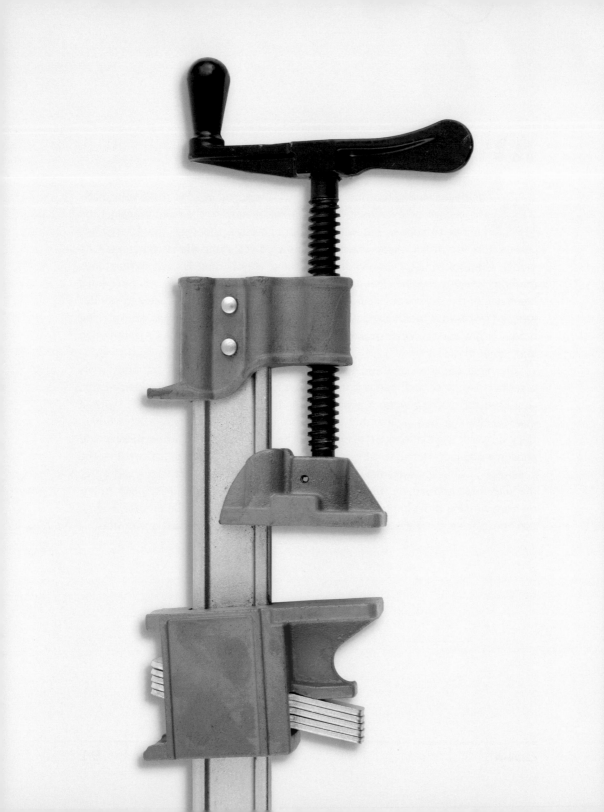

BAR CLAMP

This is the indispensable tool for clamping together pieces of wood to make a panel or for assembling furniture parts into a subassembly—say, an apron and a table leg. It's a bar of some material, typically steel. At one end of the bar is a fixed head into which is threaded a stout screw (an acme screw, to be precise, the same type of thread used on bench vises). The screw has a handle at one end and a foot at the other. Crank the screw's handle clockwise and you move the foot toward the opposite end of the clamp. A counter-clockwise movement has the opposite effect. At the other end of the bar is an adjustable stop. If you want to clamp a wide panel or a large subassembly, you move the stop down the bar, permitting a large space between it and the movable foot. Then you tighten the handle.

There are plenty of variations on this bar clamp theme. One version of the bar clamp is the K body. It reverses the locations of the head and the movable stop. With this clamp, the head is fixed and a movable stop (complete with the screw and pivoting foot) is opposite it. This has one significant advantage over the traditional design: It's easier and faster to adjust. You place the clamp in position over the workpiece and slide up the movable stop so that it makes contact. Tighten the handle and you're in business.

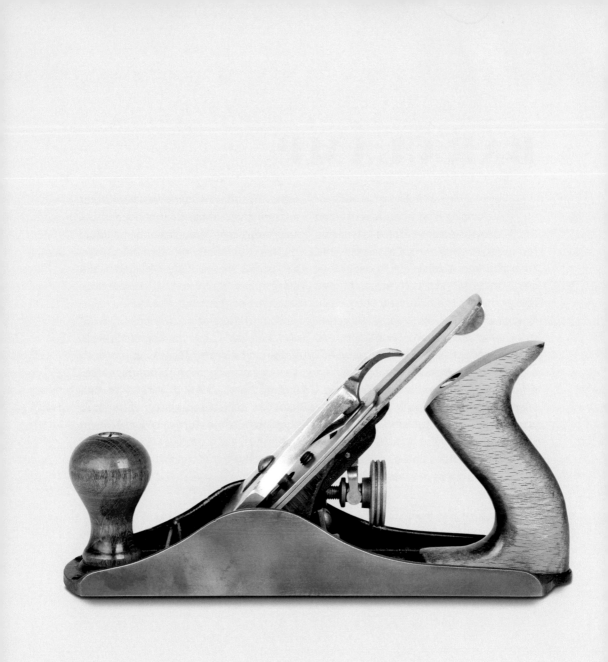

BENCH PLANE

A bench plane is the most common type of hand plane. It can be used for coarse or fine wood removal—whether you need to carefully smooth and straighten the edge of a workpiece so that it will mate up flawlessly to another or touch up the edge of a door. It also removes saw marks from a cut edge.

Hand planes come in nimble lengths of 6 inches all the way up to about 24 inches, for working really long edges. (The longer length means that the plane will correct any dips or mounds in the wood's surface. Shorter planes might follow those flaws, continuing them as you plane the wood down. But a longer plane acts as a bridge over them. After enough passes, any dip or mounds will be gone.) Learning the fine points of one is a traditional skill, but you don't have to be a master to use it. Even basic use of a sharp plane will improve the appearance and fit of your projects.

The other major types of planes are block planes (for trimming small areas as opposed to long pieces), scrub planes (when you want to take off a lot of wood quickly), and jointer planes (to get the surface of a piece of wood prepared for finishing). The more woodworking you do—and the better you get at it—the more different types of planes you'll need.

★ **WISH LIST**

STANLEY SWEETHEART NO. 4 SMOOTHING BENCH PLANE
It may look like a museum piece, but this plane is a true workshop workhorse. Reimagined for the modern woodworker, the Sweetheart No. 4 has cherry handles and an extra-thick iron, while its base and frog components are cast as a single piece to reduce chatter.

BLOCK PLANE

Block planes were specifically developed to cut end grain. These pocket-size planes are perfect for smaller jobs, fitting jobs in finish carpentry, and furniture making.

A standard block plane is often used as a one-handed cutting tool, and while it's too small to straighten boards, it is unsurpassed in making small adjustments to miters or removing saw blade marks from the edge of a board that has been ripped to width.

The block plane is engineered to cut with the grain, but it was actually conceived as a cross-grain cutting tool. The typical block plane's blade is set low at 21 degrees and makes a shallow cut, thus lowering the chance of tear-out. Low-angle block planes have the blade set at about 12 degrees and, when properly sharpened, will cut translucent ribbons of wood for amazingly precise results in furniture making, finish carpentry, and boat building. If you have to remember one thing about these planes, it's this: Unlike a larger bench plane, which operates with the cutter's bevel facing down, the bevel on a block plane's cutter faces up.

TIP!

WHAT YOUR PLANE CAN TEACH YOU

These handy tools are bursting with life lessons: remove a little stock at a time; feel the tool through the work; sharp tools work best; and more. Stanley's 12-220 is a mainstay. Scope out Lee Valley Tools or Bridge City Tool Works for higher-end items. And remember, woodworkers always lay planes on their side when they're not using them, to protect the iron's edge.

C CLAMP

What's there to say about this simple C-shaped tool? Quite a bit. Let's start at the beginning. It's a metal C with an acme-threaded rod (or spindle, to be more exact) in it. On one end of the spindle is a pivoting foot, and at the other is the handle that you turn. The spindle threads through a big hole in the lower jaw of the C. Turn the handle clockwise and you feed the threaded spindle through the bottom jaw of the C. When the foot makes contact with the workpiece, you begin applying clamping pressure between it and the top, fixed point of the C. It's a beautifully simple design.

C clamps come in two varieties. For industrial-duty work, the C is made of forged and heat-treated steel. If you are a rigger, a welder, or are clamping something in an industrial setting where you must have unquestioned strength and ultimate holding power, this is what you use. Some forged clamps don't even have a handle; the end of the spindle has a piece of forged steel shaped like a nut. You fasten a wrench onto that nut-like thing and crank for all you're worth. Most homeowners can use the less-expensive C clamp made from cast iron or malleable cast iron. This isn't as strong as a forged-steel C clamp. Then again, you're probably not holding a building's steel post and beam in position. You're probably clamping parts of a birdhouse or welding a go-kart frame. In that case, cast iron is more than strong enough.

SHOP NOTES

HOW TO BEVEL WITH A HANDSAW
Cutting a bevel the length of a board with a handsaw is not easy—but without a table saw, you may have no choice. Here's a way to ensure a uniform cut: After penciling in your cut line, clamp a 2 x 4 to the workpiece, located such that when the saw blade is rested against the 2 x 4 and aligned with the cut line, it meets the board at the angle of the bevel. Then hold the saw against the 2 x 4 as you cut.

CAULK GUN

A cheap caulk gun doesn't apply even pressure during the extrusion of the caulk and may affect the bead you're laying. Worse still, the caulk can literally backfire around the stopper, leaving you with a mess of wasted material on your hands. A good-quality gun, on the other hand, will cost from $8 to $12 and will prove its worth the first time you use it. There's nothing as expensive as cheap tools.

These guns keep steady pressure with a no-drip feature that truly works. The poker rod is actually long enough to puncture the nozzle seal on the tube of caulk, instead of making you cut the tube lower down on the nozzle than you want.

Caulk may be the most misused building product in the world. It is used to seal joints between adjacent building elements, like a tub and a wall. Unfortunately, caulk is often substituted for good workmanship or proper construction. It is not meant to fill large gaps; it's meant to ease the transition between two well-fitted building elements.

To remove old caulk, simply soften the existing caulk with a caulk remover. Then slice through the softened caulk with a sharp utility knife. The caulk should come free, but if not, a pair of needle-nose pliers will help. Rake the remaining caulk from the joint using a 5-in-1 tool. Before applying a new bead of caulk, clean the surface. If there's any mildew, a solution of $1/3$ cup of bleach to a gallon of water does the trick. Once the area is clean and dry, apply your bead of caulk.

TIP! CAULK LIKE A PROFESSIONAL

If the joint needs extra wiping to look good, draw a moistened finger down it [assuming you're using a latex or latex blend]. If you're using a caulk that requires cleanup with mineral spirits, wear a disposable nitrile glove. The glove reduces the wear and tear on your finger and will make cleanup easier when you're done. Peel the glove. Toss it out.

COPING SAW

This exacting and inexpensive saw is a gem for making intricate cuts. Taking its name from the function it provides, coping, it is the preferred method for making the inside corners of moldings look good.

The saw is designed to cut on the pull stroke, but many people set the blade to cut on the push stroke. Depending what you're cutting, there is an assortment of blades available, but most people make do with a blade with 15 tpi. Fewer teeth makes for faster sawing but a rougher cut. More teeth means a smoother cut.

The first step in coping a piece of molding is to establish your cut line. With a miter saw, cut the molding at a 45-degree angle. Make a pencil mark highlighting the molding's profile. Then back cut the piece of molding to create a mirror image of the abutting profile. It takes some practice, but when done right, your cut will mate neatly with another piece of molding like an interlocking puzzle piece.

Hold or clamp the molding down on a bench or saw horse and ease the blade of the coping saw into the wood. Don't force it. If the blade wanders away from your cut line, back it out and start again. Chances are you won't make the cut in a single run—especially with complex molding profiles. You'll probably have to ease your cut with 100-grit sandpaper or a file for a perfect fit.

SHOP NOTES

HOW TO COPE
```
Cut the first piece of molding to length and install
it so the square end abuts the adjoining wall.
Before coping the next piece, cut an inside miter
at 45 degrees to expose the molding's profile. For cutting
miters in sprung crown, build a plywood jig that holds the
crown upside down and mimics the wall-to-ceiling junction.
Using a coping saw, cut along the front edge of the miter.
Be sure to tilt the saw blade a few degrees back from
perpendicular to the face of the molding. Position the
molding in place or against some scrap to test-fit the
join. Clean up with sandpaper, a file, or a utility knife.
```

CROSSCUT SAW

ven if you own an arsenal of power saws, an eight-point cross-cut saw should have a place of honor in your shop. It may not make the finest cuts, but it's the perfect jack-of-all-trades saw for small jobs, like that occasional 2 x 4.

To make a cut, mark your line and cut to the waste side. Start your cut by drawing the saw lightly backward while holding it at a shallow angle to get the blade started. Use the thumb of the hand that's holding the board as a guide, and hold the saw so its toothed edge is at an approximately 45-degree angle to the work surface. Push the saw forward, using full strokes and as much of the blade as possible. You're cutting with the push stroke, so don't bear down on the saw; it'll just slow you down. Let the saw cut the wood.

As you complete the cut, lower the angle of the saw to minimize splintering the cut on the board's bottom. Make sure the final draw is a slow, backward pull.

And one more tip: if the kerf (the rut your saw creates in the wood) closes on the blade, jamming you up, slip a 16d common nail into the kerf to hold it open.

DON'T SKIMP ON YOUR CROSSCUT SAW

TIP! If you're looking for the perfect pegboard centerpiece, we recommend either Lee Valley's Wenzloff Cross-cut Panel Saw or Thomas Flinn & Co.'s PAX Panel Saw. Neither are cheap, but their classic design, hand-sharpened spring-steel blades, wood handles, and taper-ground precision will make you wonder why you didn't upgrade earlier.

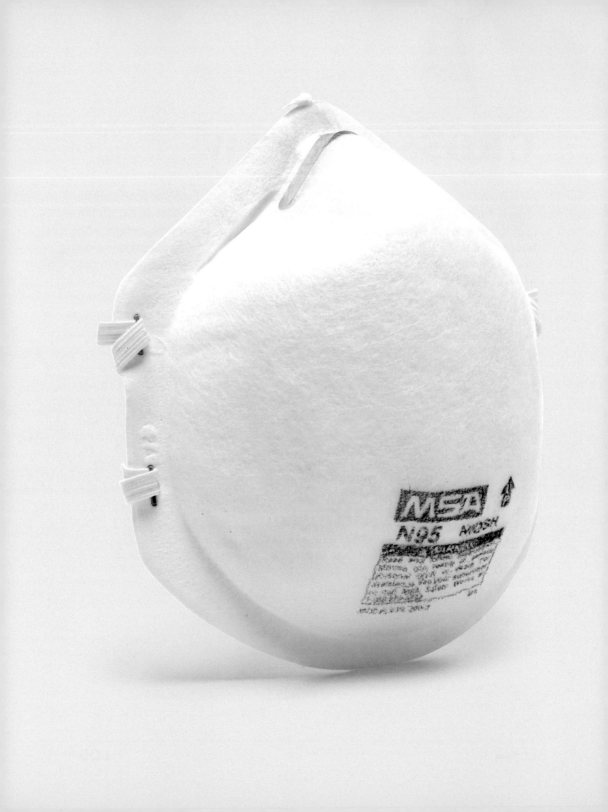

DUST MASK

A dust mask provides protection against nontoxic dust and pollen and is an irreplaceable tool for anyone with a workshop. A step up are respirators, which provide protection against fumes, gases, vapors, and other harmful particles in the air.

How do you tell the difference? An inexpensive dust mask lacks a rating by NIOSH and will not seal tightly against your face, allowing airborne hazards to enter your airway. For most jobs, use a disposable respirator. Respirators will have a NIOSH rating; many are given an N95 rating, which means that they are rated to filter out fine particles like soot, smoke, and ash and have a 95 percent efficiency rating against solid and liquid particles that don't contain oil. An N100 rating is even better. Sometimes Web-based retailers and others call both products by the same name, so shop carefully.

If you're sanding drywall compound, refinishing a floor, cutting cedar or black walnut, or performing any other job that creates airborne dust, then you need to protect your lungs. Although you're using a respirator, you might not have fitted it against your face properly. If you have a beard or a couple of days' growth, the mask will not form a tight seal and particles can enter your airway. To make sure the mask is fitted properly, cover your respirator with both hands but don't press it against your face. Exhale sharply. If you feel air blowing on your face or eyes, the respirator needs to be adjusted.

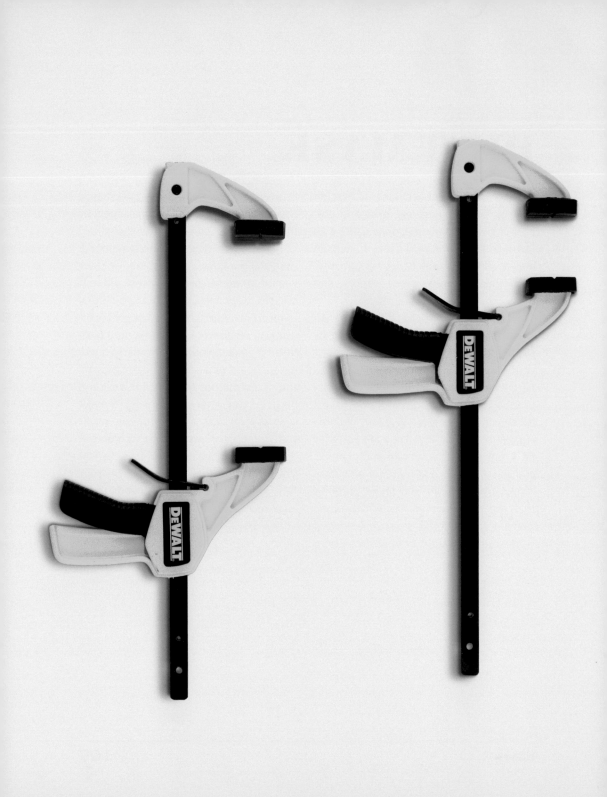

FAST-ACTION CLAMP

You learn pretty early on in construction and woodworking that you're constrained by the fact that you have only two hands. Seriously, there are times when you need to hold something with one hand and clamp it with the other. There's no time for formalities or fiddling around with attaching typical clamps. You need to clamp that piece of wood so you can saw or drill it.

The tool that you turn to is the king of rapid-deployment clamps: the fast-action. It's equipped with a pistol grip handle and a spring-loaded catch that enables you to move the tool quickly into position with one hand. Hook its head in place, put the moveable jaw where you want it, and then squeeze the pistol grip to tighten. Done. To release the tool, press on the spring-loaded latch, and presto, you're on to your next clamping assignment.

The tool is nothing more than two plastic heads riding on a steel bar. Some have the thoughtful feature of being able to reverse the direction of the clamp heads. This enables you to spread something apart with gentle but firm force, which is useful in furniture restoration, since it gives you damage-free disassembly.

TIP!

YET ANOTHER CLAMP
A close cousin to the fast-acting clamp is the wooden cam clamp. It has wooden jaws with cork pads and a cam lever that applies a modest amount of pressure.

MARKING GAUGE

The marking gauge is a traditionalist's tool that has quirky benefits for non-traditional woodworkers. Its wooden or steel bar has a hardened steel pin embedded in it. You can adjust the fence relative to the pin and lock it down at an appropriate distance. When you slide the fence along the edge of a workpiece, the pin scribes a line parallel to that edge. It works on both wood and metal.

Why do you need this? Let's say you want to cut a traditional tenon (a rectangular peg that fits into a rectangular hole called a mortise). It's faster to do this with machines, but if you need only three or four, then hand tools will do just fine. Using the marking gauge to mark the tenon and the mortise will ensure that they match. Or maybe you want a neat line of screws to fall parallel to one edge of your workpiece. The marking gauge can mark their location—and people who see your work will stand back and wonder how you did it.

If you want to up your traditional woodworking game, you can also buy a mortise marking gauge. It scores two parallel lines to a surface at the same time. That way, you can mark lines for both surfaces of a mortise or tenon or make two perfectly parallel rows of screws.

SHOP NOTES

HOW TO MAKE AN ADJUSTABLE MARKING GAUGE FROM A DRYWALL SCREW

Make a quick-and-dirty version by driving a drywall screw into a scrap of wood. The outside edge of the screwhead acts as the marking blade. Adjust the distance simply by turning the screw. For better results, sharpen the edge of the screwhead with a sanding block. We'd never use this tool for setting up dovetails, but it's fine for creating reference marks on a door jam prior to installing casing.

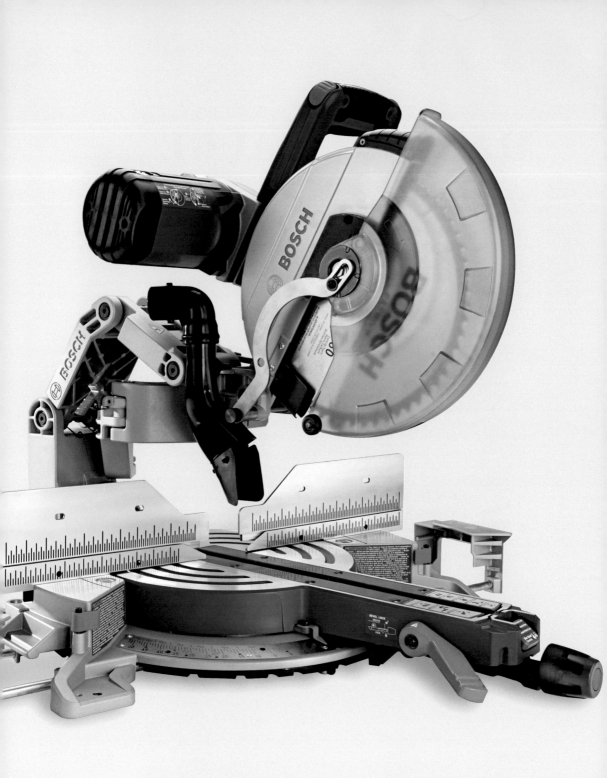

MITER SAW

A miter saw is also called a chop saw because the blade comes down into the workpiece like a karate chop. It is a portable precision instrument that every trim carpenter or woodworker must own.

Which saw is right for you depends on what you're going to do. If you plan on cutting wide crown, baseboard, 2 x 10s, or 4x stock, then a 12-inch sliding compound miter saw is the one you'll want to own.

But if you're using it mostly for smaller stock, a minisliding compound miter saw may be exactly what you need. It features a 7¼-inch blade and has an 11¾-inch crosscut capacity and the ability to cut a 2 x 8 at 45 degrees. While this saw will not cut through 4x stock or wide crown moldings, it is much lighter than the 10- or 12-inch models.

Direct-drive miter saws have the motor in line with the blade and are the least expensive saws available. But with a direct-drive saw, the motor's vibrations transfer directly to the blade and may cost you some precision in your cuts. Direct-drive saws are perfect for plumbing, flooring, and landscaping work.

With a belt-driven saw, the blade isn't affected by the motor's vibration. These saws offer a consistent cutting depth on either side of the blade. The motor sits back out of the way and lets you make a compound miter on either side of the blade. A belt-driven saw is preferred for making furniture, built-ins, and fireplace mantels and for other finish carpentry tasks where precision is a must.

And one more thing: buy or make a stand for this saw. Crawling around on the floor trying to eye a careful miter is no way to work.

NAIL SET

A nail set allows you to counter-sink nailheads without damaging the surrounding surface, then conceal the holes with wood filler. The nail set should fit the finishing nail's head so you can set the nail without making a hole larger than the nailhead.

The head of a finishing nail has a slight concavity, and that's where to seat the nail set. Align the set with the shank of the nail, and, using a 16-ounce hammer, strike the set until you've sunk the nail about ⅛ inch below the wood's surface.

One or two whacks ought to do it. Hard cap nail sets have a large plastic striking surface and an easy-to-grip shank, making it an easier tool to use.

Nail sets are handy if you use a nail gun, too. Sometimes the nail gun doesn't countersink the fastener. You can sink a pneumatic nail the same way you sink an old-fashioned finishing nail, but with the pneumatic kind, you won't find an easy-to-seat dimple to help you out. Instead, you'll have to balance the set on the nail's head and tap it.

TIP!

BIGGER IS OKAY
While you can use a set that's one size larger than you need, don't try to use an undersize one—this can damage the tool's cup-shaped tip. To ensure you've got the right size, get a set of four: ¹⁄₃₂-, ¹⁄₁₆-, ³⁄₃₂-, and ⅛-inch.

PAINTBRUSH/ ROLLER

Don't be cheap when you're buying paintbrushes or roller covers. The bristles or fibers will come off on the wall, leaving you with a disappointing finish. Purdy is a good brand.

For most jobs, you want a 2½-inch sash brush, which lets you cut in on corners and around trim. Synthetic bristles are best for latex paints, and natural bristles work better with oil-based paints.

When selecting a roller cover, pay attention to its nap, or the length of the cover's fibers. On a smooth wall, you'll use a shorter-napped roller cover, like a ¼-inch to ⅜-inch nap, and for stucco or brick, a longer nap, like ¾- to 1-inch. Cardboard roller cores won't last very long, since they absorb moisture and lose roundness. Get plastic instead.

To clean a brush of latex paint, first scrape off excess paint, then rinse in lukewarm water with the bristles facing down. Dip the brush in a bucket of soapy water and swirl it around, making sure not to bend the bristles against the bottom. Repeat if necessary. When the brush is clean, wrap the bristles in a paper towel to wick away a lot of the water. As the paper towel dries, it shrinks and helps keep the shape of the brush. Remember to never lean a drying brush on the bristles.

To clean a roller, use the arched edge of a 5-in-1 painter's tool to scrape as much paint from it as you can. Then run it under lukewarm water using the 5-in-1 as a squeegee until the paint is removed. Stand it on end, placing it on a folded paper towel, and let dry.

TIP!

HOW TO KEEP YOUR PAINT ROLLER FROM DRYING OUT
If you have to pause a painting job, wrap your roller and brushes tightly in a plastic bag and stick them in the freezer. Once thawed, they'll be ready to use. Just be sure to seal the bag tightly to eliminate any chance of food contamination.

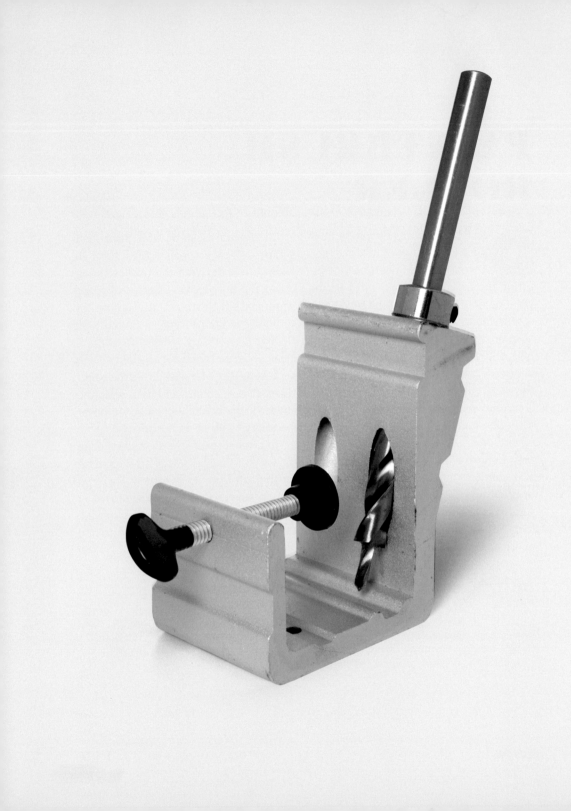

POCKET HOLE JIG

A pocket hole jig is a tool for making quick, strong joints in wood. Whether you're a weekend warrior or a bona fide artisan woodworker, this tool will not only help you get great results when building cabinets, bookcases, entertainment centers, and the like, but it will also deliver these results almost immediately.

A pocket hole jig allows you to drill a hole at a very shallow angle into a piece of wood. A screw is then driven through this hole and into an adjoining piece of wood to create a tight, strong joint. Because the hole is drilled on a shallow angle, the screw won't protrude out of the other board and a significant amount of the screw's threading is centered on the joint. It's fast and strong, and you don't have to wait around for the glue to dry.

The jig is one part of the equation; the other is a stepped drill bit. A stepped drill bit does two jobs simultaneously. First, it bores a hole large enough to accommodate the screwhead. Then, because it's stepped, the thinner tip bores a pilot hole for the screw to follow, so it won't split your workpiece. Prices range from $6 for an entry level model (remember, you get what you pay for) to $100 for something more suited to a professional.

⭐ **WISH LIST**

THE BEST POCKET HOLE JIG COMES AT A PREMIUM

For the dedicated carpenter with money to burn, there's the Kreg line of electric and pneumatic power tools, sure to give you a perfect pocket hole each and every time. Some of these models are much pricier than the handheld options [one that performs five pocket holes at once is close to five figures], but working with an automatic jig can be a real time-saver.

PUTTY KNIFE

The putty knife is more than a single implement. Rather, it's a group of tools, ranging from knives with flexible, thin blades to heavy-duty models that are ground with a tip like a chisel (which, not surprisingly, are called chisel-edge putty knives).

You can get by with owning just one or two. A thinner 1-inch-wide stiff blade works wonders on jobs like glazing windows and filling nail holes, while a more flexible 4-inch-wide knife comes in really handy for small dry wall repairs, such as smoothing out a ding from a child's thrown toy.

A 1-inch blade typically has a chisel-shaped bevel point (pictured) and a thick ($\frac{5}{64}$-inch) high-carbon steel blade. The flexible 4-inch skiff has a thinner blade ($\frac{5}{32}$-inch) but is still made of high-carbon steel.

Never apply wood filler with your finger, because it will mold to the wood's surface, announcing the nail hole instead of concealing it. Instead, use the 1-inch knife to apply the putty and then remove the excess putty by drawing the blade in the opposite direction of application. If you're working on a wood surface that is going to be stained, reach for a flexible-bladed putty knife, especially when working with softer woods like pine or cedar. With a flexible blade, you're less likely to damage a fragile surface.

Better tools have a high-carbon steel blade. Reserve using those plastic disposable ones for working with a two-part auto body filler, the no-scuff application of putty on painted surfaces, or an epoxy reserved for exterior repairs, such as porch columns or window sills that have suffered some rot.

SHOP NOTES

HOW TO USE A PUTTY KNIFE TO PROTECT YOUR WALL
Tired of scuffing or scratching a surface when removing nails? Slide a putty knife under a nail before using a claw hammer to remove it. The hammer rolls against the knife, preserving the surface.

RANDOM ORBITAL SANDER

If you are in the market to buy just one sander, pick up a random orbital sander. This tool combines orbital motion with rotation and, when armed with the right sandpaper, can handle almost any job requiring abrasive action, from stripping paint to producing a nearly mirror finish on wood or metal. If you've got a lot of material to remove, use a belt sander.

Random orbital sanders come in three sizes. Palm sanders are for light-duty finish work. A pistol grip sander is for heavier work. Large right-angle sanders are for smoothing large surfaces, like floors and tabletops. Many models offer variable speeds as well as orbit modes for fine finishing or more aggressive action.

Look for a tool that has a vacuum adapter so you can connect it to your shop vac. This is a great addition to the tool, since you're significantly reducing airborne hazards by directing the dust into the shop vac instead of letting it settle all over the place. While just about every random orbital sander does have a dust bag, they are no match for a vacuum attachment.

TIP!

HOW TO CHOOSE SANDING DISKS
In addition to the vacuum adapter, you'll need to select which of two sanding disks best suits your needs. We recommend going with the hook-and-loop system over the pressure-sensitive adhesive disc. The hook-and-loop, while a bit more expensive, allows the user to quickly and easily switch grits and reuse discs that aren't yet worn out.

ROUTER

Routers are one of the most popular woodworking tools around for making dadoes and dovetails and performing any number of joinery operations, as well as adding a decorative flair to the edge of a surface, such as a shelf or tabletop.

The first thing to consider when shopping for a router is horsepower. Horsepower determines the work that the machine can do and the diameter of the bits it can handle. General-purpose routers are 1 to 2 horsepower, whereas heavy-duty routers used in cabinet shops usually rate 3 horsepower or better.

The most versatile of these handheld tools is the D-handle router. The D-handle configuration is easy to grab, and the on/off switch is under your index finger, like a trigger. There will be no more fumbling for the toggle switch while the tool in your hand spins at 10,000 rpm.

Typically, routers come with ¼-inch and ½-inch collets, or sleeves that hold router bits. Whenever possible, stick with the ½-inch collets and bits. The ½-inch bits are eight times stronger than the smaller bits and cut smoother, especially in hardwoods and sheet goods.

The D-handle is the go-to setup for a fixed base. A plunge base lets you do all the things a fixed base does, plus it lets you alter the depth of the cut on the fly. The plunge base safely lowers the bit into the wood instead of having to start at the board's edge—perfect for making mortises or decorative columns for your house.

When buying a router, get a kit with at least two of these three bases: a plunge, fixed, and D-handle. It costs a bit more at first, but it gives you the freedom to tackle a number of jobs with one tool.

SHARPENING STONES

If you want to have a chance at being a good woodworker, you need sharp tools. Sharpening stones come in two types. Combination stones have a coarse side and a relatively fine side. Dedicated grits are the same on both sides, and they allow you to sharpen with more precision. The most common stones are rectangular slabs. Most are made from industrial abrasives that are fused together at high temperatures, producing a synthetic stone. But some natural stones are still sold. Arkansas stones are famous for their hardness and long-wearing ability. You can own an Arkansas stone for years and never wear it out.

Whether manmade or natural, sharpening stones have a top layer of abrasive particles that are sacrificed in order to wear away the steel being sharpened on them. Also, they're porous. This is important because you need some sort of sharpening medium, such as water or oil, to carry away the metal particles. (That's what sharpening is: wearing away the dull metal to produce sharp metal.)

Stones are defined by coarseness. They may be labeled simply as "coarse" or "fine" or given numbers similar to sandpaper. When sharpening, always move from stones that are designated as coarse to those that are fine.

SHOP NOTES

HOW TO SHARPEN A KNIFE

A knife may be the most elemental of all human tools—but only if it's sharp. Hone it with a steady hand and a combination stone that has a coarse and fine side. The trick is to hold the blade at the correct angle. Bob Montagno, an expert sharpener and plant manager at Norton Pike [the first American sharpening-stone maker], suggests to lubricate the coarse side with mineral oil or water; then push the blade across in a sweeping motion. "Flip the knife and work the other side until a slight burr forms," Montagno says. "Switch to the fine side of the stone, lift the blade to a slightly higher angle and hone off the burr to create a razor-sharp micro bevel."

SHOULDER PLANE

On a perfect day, you use machines and power tools for woodworking and end up with tools that fit precisely together, without fine-tuning. But most days aren't perfect. For those days, you might need a shoulder plane. This precision woodworking tool has been refined over thousands of years. It has a cutter that somewhat resembles a chisel. The cutter projects to the very outside edges of the plane body, allowing you to plane into corners. This comes in handy when, say, you're fitting a cabinet door in a recess that forms a stop but you need to remove just a hair from that recess in order for the door to close with a satisfyingly crisp action (and look perfect from the outside). Or maybe you're fitting together a piece of furniture with traditional wood joints. It's not unusual for the joints themselves to need tweaking so that the parts can go together just so.

As for the name itself, a shoulder is a part of a wood tenon. While fitting a tenon into a mortise, you'll often have to pare the tenon's shoulder back just a hair. The best way to do that? With your trusted shoulder plane.

SHOP NOTES

HOW TO MAKE A FLEXIBLE SANDING BLOCK
A rigid wood sanding block can be a handicap if a surface isn't flat. When dealing with a subtle curve, stack sheets of corrugated cardboard and wrap them in sandpaper, like a normal block. The cardboard has some give, so it'll hug the curve.

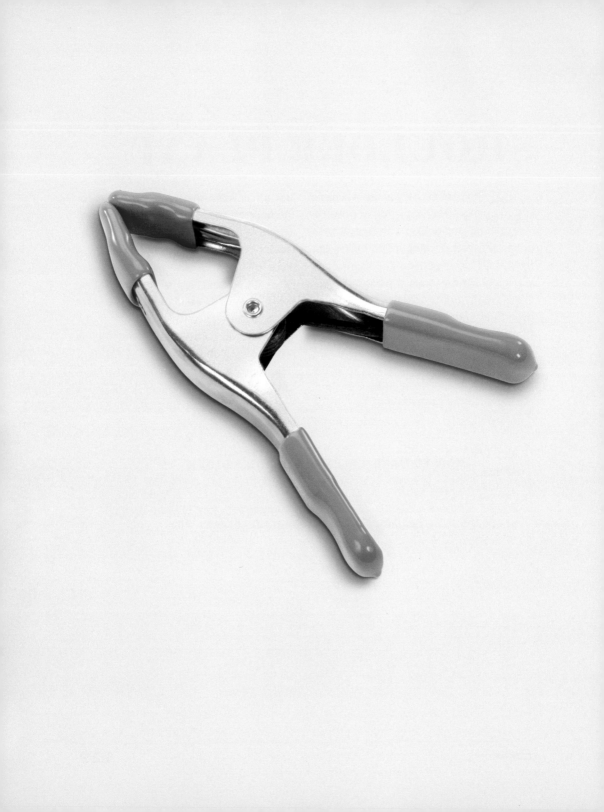

SPRING CLAMP

The other clamps included in this book (Bar Clamp, page 93; C Clamp, page 99; and Fast-Action Clamp, page 109) are designed to provide variable clamping power. But there will be many moments in your workshop when you don't need much in the way of power, or even reach. You simply need quick, one-handed placement in any position, especially a tight spot. In those moments, what you need is a simple spring clamp.

This clamp is nothing more than two stamped sheet steel halves connected by a spring. It looks like the letter A. Bear down on the handles and you move the jaws apart. Place the clamp in position and let go of the handle and the jaws apply pressure on the workpiece. The rubberized tips on the jaws help produce a sure, slip-free grip on the surface of the workpiece. Just remember: They don't have a very tight grip, and they don't open very far. These little gems are handy as can be in woodworking and trim carpentry, where you've got to hold small blocks or strips of wood in place rapidly and, often, with one hand on the clamp and the other on the wood. Or maybe you're holding down something like a tarp. You'll find uses for them that you never imagined. And some that we haven't, either. You can never have too many. Luckily, spring clamps are relatively inexpensive, so you won't feel bad for buying as many as you want.

SHOP NOTES

USE BOTTLE CAPS TO PROTECT CLAMPED SURFACES
If you're clamping a surface and are worried the clamp isn't sufficiently padded to keep it from marring the surface, try putting a bottle cap between the clamp and the workpiece.

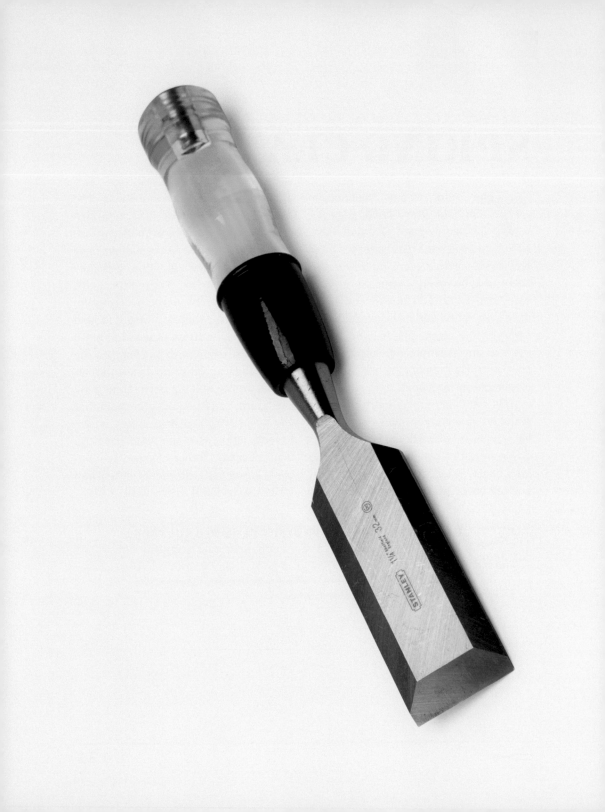

WOOD CHISEL

For proper cutting, the back of the wood chisel must be perfectly flat and the beveled edge has to be sharp. Using a chisel is not difficult, and with a little practice, you'll be mortising hinges or repairing damaged trim details like a pro.

To mortise a hinge, trace the hinge onto the door or jamb. With the chisel, score the outline, making sure to keep the beveled face of the chisel toward the mortise. You'll only want to score to the depth of the hinge. Once the outline is finished, make a series of shallow cuts across the grain about every quarter of an inch or so. Gently tap the chisel and be aware of your depth as you cut. Once you've made your crosscuts, take out the wood between them using the chisel, bevel side down. Finish paring the bottom of the mortise flat with the bevel side up.

Some wood chisels have a metal shaft, or tang, that runs from the large steel striking cap all the way to the blade. This makes for a stronger chisel, and when you strike it with a hammer, very little of the force gets absorbed by the handle. This type of chisel is a stronger tool and can be used for the most rugged chopping in carpentry, furniture construction, and boat building.

When you're looking for your set, we recommend picking up at least four: a ¼-, ½-, ¾- and 1-inch. These four chisels will last you a lifetime if cared for properly.

To hone a chisel, work the bevel over a sharpening stone so that you form a burr on its tip (known as the wire edge). Flip it over, then hone the back, removing the wire edge in the process. One or two more strokes on the bevel, then one or two on the back, and you're done.

Farmhouse Table

There's no better way to give thanks than by gathering family and friends around an enormous table to share a feast. And a farmhouse table is the perfect spot. You can make one out of construction lumber and ordinary hardware in a couple of days. We're not talking precision woodworking here. If you can handle a circular saw and a chisel, you can do this. Farmers used to build these tables themselves, not furniture makers or carpenters, so it's okay if it turns out a bit rustic. That's half the fun. The other half is sitting down to eat at a table you built yourself.

Materials

PART	DESCRIPTION	QTY	LUMBER	LENGTH
A	Tabletop piece	3	2" x 12"	61"
B	Breadboard end	2	2" x 6"	34"
C	Leg	4	4" x 4"	24½"
D	Short stretcher	2	4" x 4"	26"
E	Long stretcher	1	2" x 4"	56½"
F	Short apron	2	2" x 4"	18¾"
G	Long apron	2	2" x 4"	49"

Instructions

STEP 1: PREP YOUR LUMBER

(1) Construction lumber has a higher moisture content than the wood used to build furniture, so after purchasing it, let it sit inside your house for several weeks to dry it out a little.

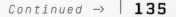

Continued →

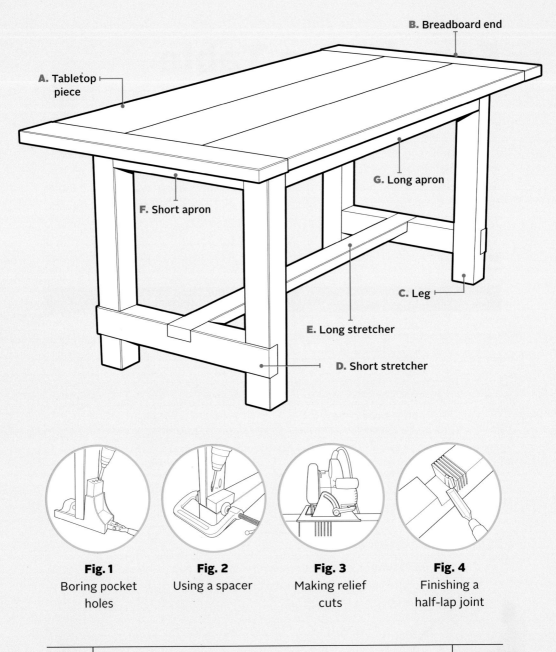

A. Tabletop piece

B. Breadboard end

G. Long apron

F. Short apron

C. Leg

E. Long stretcher

D. Short stretcher

Fig. 1
Boring pocket holes

Fig. 2
Using a spacer

Fig. 3
Making relief cuts

Fig. 4
Finishing a half-lap joint

② To start, you'll want to cut out the pieces. Crosscut the top pieces, breadboard ends, stretchers, and legs. Note that the breadboard ends are slightly wider than the tabletop. This is a rustic detail with a practical aspect. It will allow the top to expand and contract with humidity and never be wider than the breadboard ends. There is also a slight overhang on the stretchers, for a similar reason. When you cut the legs, double-check that the length is a good fit for your dining-room chairs, especially if any of them have arms. Chairs with arms should be able to easily slide under the table's aprons.

③ Crosscut both short aprons, but don't cut the long aprons. You'll measure those after joining the legs and stretchers.

STEP 2: CREATE THE BASE

① To start, make a base assembly out of the aprons, legs, and stretchers. Attach one leg on either side of one of the short aprons. Bore two holes for pocket screws into each side of the apron's back, four in total (**Fig. 1**). Clamp the legs at the apron, but add a ⅛-inch piece of wood to the front as a spacer (**Fig. 2**). This will offset the face of the apron from the face of the leg, pushing it back a bit and creating a nice dimensionality. Drive the pocket screws through the apron into the leg. Repeat the same procedure for the second leg-apron assembly.

② You're going to connect the two leg-apron assemblies to the stretchers using cross lap joints. These are among the easiest and most forgiving of wood joints to make, and they're also quite sturdy. Mark the joint positions on the legs and stretchers. Start the half-lap joints on the legs by notching the two outside lines

TIP! When buying lumber for furniture, even if it's construction-grade, you may have to cut the best piece from a larger hunk of wood. After you choose the lumber from the stack, use chalk to mark the outline of the board you want. Then remove the excess. Yes, this results in more waste, but your finished product will look better for it.

Continued →

with a circular saw set to a depth of 1½ inches. Guide the saw using a triangular rafter square. Between the two outside cuts make a series of relief cuts spaced ⅛-inch apart (**Fig. 3**). Then use a sharp chisel to chop away the waste (**Fig. 4**). When you cut the half-lap joints on the short stretcher, set the saw's depth to 1⅜ inches deep. This will make the stretcher extend ⅝-inch past the surface of the leg when the table is finally assembled. The offset will give you a table that looks like it was built by a farmer rather than by west elm. It'll look nice.

③ Before connecting the pieces, follow the same procedure to cut a 3½-inch-wide x 1⅜-inch-deep notch in the middle of each short stretcher. This is where the long stretcher will sit.

④ Spread glue on the notched face of the short stretcher and the notched face of the leg, and press the pieces together. Make a counterbored hole through the leg's back and into the stretcher. Drive a 2½-inch coarse-thread pocket screw through the leg into the stretcher to lock the pieces together. To hide the hole, glue a dowel into it, trim it flush with a chisel, and sand it smooth.

STEP 3: ASSEMBLE

① Glue the long stretcher into its notches on the short stretchers, and check that the two leg subassemblies are standing square to it. Counterbore screw holes in the long stretcher's end, and drive the screws to fasten it. Now measure and crosscut the long aprons. Join the long aprons to the leg subassemblies using pocket screws.

② To make the top, align the three pieces of 2 x 12. Fit them as tightly together as you can. Bore four pocket-screw holes through the bottom faces of the

FINISH IT
Chairs don't match your new table? Try one of these Minwax oil-based wood finish colors.

Natural
209

Sedona Red
222

Dark Walnut
2716

top pieces, then spread glue on each adjoining edge. With the pieces clamped together so that the ends are flush, fasten with 2½-inch pocket screws. Glue will squeeze out of the joint. Wait a few minutes for the glue to get rubbery, then shave it off with a chisel. Keep the top flat as it dries—we like to clamp cauls across both ends to add stability. (Cauls are 2 x 4s or other pieces of stout wood turned on their edges.)

(3) It's important that the ends of the top are straight and square. If the top shifts as the glue dries, trim it with a saw, using the breadboard ends as a guide.

(4) Use a doweling jig to bore holes in the ends of the tabletop and on one side of each breadboard piece. After test-fitting the breadboard ends, spread a little glue on the dowels, attach the ends, then use three ratchet-strap clamps to apply pressure as the glue dries.

(5) Next, use right-angle brackets to mount the tabletop to the base. Elongate the bracket holes in the top a bit to allow for the wood to expand and contract with changes in humidity.

(6) Sand the table smooth. Start with 80-grit paper, and move to a finer grit for each pass. You should end with 220-grit. We finished the table with two coats of Jacobean-tinted polyurethane, then buffed on a couple of coats of wax after it was dry. The dark tint hides any scratches or nicks and also makes it look like it was built a century ago. On that note, you can give up your coasters—a little wear will only make your table look better.

TIP! If you like our table but want something that looks a little more polished, just expand the finishing step. Start by sanding carefully and thoroughly, then apply a pre-stain wood conditioner. This will highlight the wood's grain and prevent the stain from absorbing unevenly. Apply your chosen finish in thin coats, carefully sanding out each coat and removing the sanding dust with a tack cloth before applying the next one. Finish the table with a coat of wax. There, now it's shiny.

LANDSCAPING

Bow Rake..................................143

Bow Saw...................................145

Chain Saw.................................147

Garden Trowel......................149

Hand Truck...........................151

Lopper....................................153

Pick Axe.................................155

Post-Hole Digger.............157

Pruner....................................159

Rope.......................................161

Round Nose Shovel...........163

Square Nose Shovel.........165

Wheelbarrow......................167

BOW RAKE

Rugged and simple, the bow rake remains the best device for raking heavy material, such as gravel or tangled sticks. The bow acts as a shock absorber, protecting your arms while you work. If you turn it over, the straight back can also be used to level soil.

A bow rake's head can range in size from 8 to 24 inches in width. The head is connected to the handle with a steel bow that gives the tool some strength for serious raking. The head will have anywhere from 12 to 24 tines that are designed for leveling materials, spreading mulch or compost, blending fertilizer into tilled soil, or removing heavier debris.

To keep the tool tuned, make sure it is hosed off after being used. One precaution to take is to apply a spritz of WD-40 from time to time to keep rust at bay. And to protect a wooden handle, some Thompson's WaterSeal around the rake head is a great precaution to stave off wood rot. Fiberglass is really the way to go with these rakes, since it's light and nearly impervious to water damage.

> **TIP!**
>
> ## EVEN MORE RAKES!
> Everyone should have a bow rake on hand, but it's far from the only rake you'll need. Stock a 24-inch leaf rake to help manage your yard come autumn. And there's the compact 8-inch shrub rake if you have shrubberies, fences, or other tight spaces. Finally, a thatch rake, similar in build to the bow rake, is irreplaceable when removing thatch.

BOW SAW

The bow saw is a pruning tool for cutting branches that are less than 10 inches in diameter. The saw makes quick work of getting through a branch because the ribbon-thin blade has an aggressive set of teeth. Based on a design by the Sandvik Group out of Sweden in the 1950s, these tough, lightweight, and inexpensive saws cut quickly. They are the tool of choice for many landscapers and homeowners, as well as hunters who need to make a duck blind or clear small branches for a tree stand.

Pruning a branch takes a bit of know-how. To prune a good-size branch, you must first undercut it about 6 to 12 inches from the trunk. This cut, a relief cut really, should only go a fourth to a third of the way through the branch. Then, start the top cut about 2 inches past the undercut, away from the trunk. Depending on the size of the branch, it may snap off before you've completed your through cut. Don't worry if you've got a ragged, jagged, or fractured branch on your hands. You've got a sizable stub that you can easily and neatly cut. Don't cut too close to the trunk, though. On most trees, there's a little swell around the branch where it meets the trunk, as if the branch were coming out of a sleeve. That's called the branch collar. You always want to make your final cut just beyond the branch collar to ensure the tree's health.

While a bow saw is safer than a chain saw for removing tree limbs while standing on a ladder, it's not the tool to use if you've got some trees to drop or storm damage to clean up. For those kinds of jobs, a chain saw is your best friend.

CHAIN SAW

You have two choices on powering this irreplaceable logging tool. If you've got smaller jobs close to home, an electric saw might be your best choice. An electric version is lighter, quieter, and cleaner than its gas-powered counterpart. There's a tradeoff, though. It's not nearly as powerful, and it's simply not suited for heavy work, because it's tethered to an exterior outlet by an extension cord.

Select a gas chain saw for most jobs. A saw with an engine in the 30- to 40-cc range with an 18-inch bar is perfect for cutting up winter-damaged storm limbs and landscape maintenance work, and it will do just fine for preparing small amounts of firewood. For heavy cutting, you'll need a saw in the 55- to 60-cc range, equipped with a bar from 18 to 22 inches.

Most importantly, don't skimp on the safety gear. Get protective earmuffs, chaps, leather work gloves, and wrap-around eye protection.

Other tools and accessories that can make woodcutting more productive and safer are felling wedges (pounded into a felling cut, they push a tree over), log hooks, and two-person timber carriers. Also consider a traditional logging tool: the cant hook, or the pointed version of that tool, the peavey. Both are extremely useful for turning and positioning difficult logs. We vote thumbs-down on one logging tool: the steel saw buck, which is obviously a disaster if you hit it with a saw chain. Instead, build your own saw buck out of pressure-treated lumber. Hit that with the chain and it's no big deal.

GARDEN TROWEL

The tool that makes your garden grow is a trowel, a small, single-handed shovel. It's nothing more than a scoop-shaped blade stamped from stainless or carbon steel fastened to a wood or plastic handle. More expensive versions, usually from England or elsewhere in Europe, consist of a forged-steel blade and a polished hardwood handle. You're not going to find one of those at a hardware store. They need to be ordered from a garden supply catalog.

Whether expensive or inexpensive, either version of the tool helps you plant bulbs and small plants, dig out weeds, mix potting soil with amendments, and transfer a plant from one pot to another or from the pot to the ground. There's really not much to trowels, but you do have to take care of them. Scrub hardened clods of dirt off their blades after use. If you remove a dying plant, disinfect the tool afterward. You can buy horticultural disinfectant, but you can also use a diluted solution of household bleach (10 percent bleach, 90 percent water). After cleaning the tool, rinse it and dry it since the chlorides are highly corrosive.

SHOP NOTES

HOW TO FIX LOOSE HANDLES
It's not unusual for a riveted handle to loosen, whether it's on a kitchen knife, a garden trowel, or a long-handled shovel. Tightening the loose handle is easy. With the tool on a firm surface, strike the center of the handle rivet with a centerpunch driven by a ball-peen hammer. Don't hit it very hard, just enough to leave a small dimple. This expands the rivet slightly, taking up the slack between it and the handle.

HAND TRUCK

Once you own a hand truck, you'll wonder how you ever got along without it. If you find yourself carrying heavy things with some frequency and needing to be mobile at the same time, then you'll find this tool irreplaceable. The only downside to owning one is similar to owning a pickup truck: it's going to earn you a lot of new "friends." Especially when those friends are moving and could use some help.

Some hand trucks are small, lightweight, collapsible models, terrific for small loads like briefcases and camera equipment, and are occasionally found at airports used by frequent travelers hauling heavy luggage. But what about the serial remodeler? Tool totes and boxes get heavy pretty quickly, as do table saws and chop saws. While many manufacturers make tools that have wheels, many of us own tools that don't, and these are awkward to carry. Some are just downright heavy. Strapping them down to a hand truck makes them easy to set up and break down—and at the end of a fast-paced day in the sun, wouldn't it be nice to roll the tools back to the shop rather than being forced to carry them?

Damaged knees and compromised backs are no strangers to hands-on types, and a hand truck is a commonsense addition to anyone who has injured them or to those wanting to avoid such problems in the future. Pick up the model that would work best for you. We suggest taking an inventory of your workshop to weigh the heaviest item you'll require a hand truck for.

SHOP NOTES

MAKE YOUR HAND TRUCK SAFER

On an incline, a hand truck can roll backward and cause an injury. Reduce the risk by mounting stout fabric straps on the truck's frame, above the wheels. Move forward and the straps flap out of the way. Go backward and the straps tuck under the wheels to arrest motion.

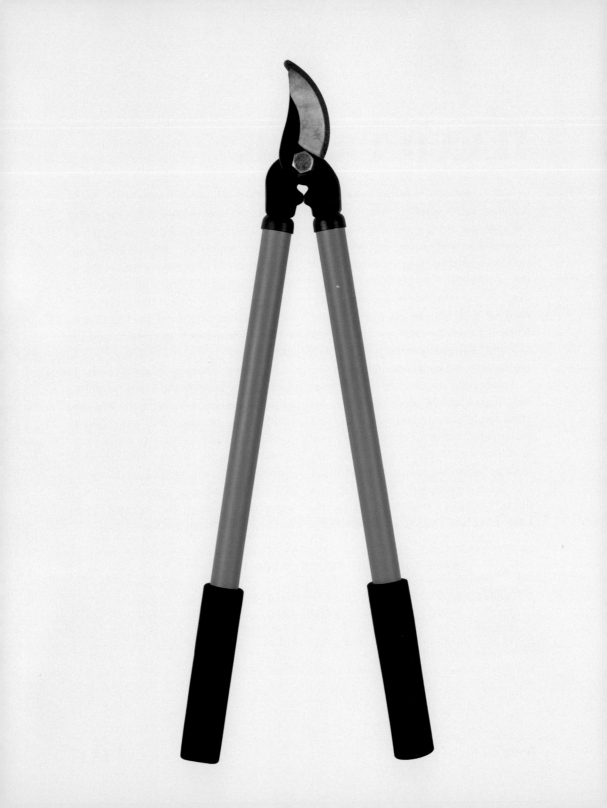

LOPPER

Chainsaws are overkill for small branches and may well whip them back at you rather than cut them. And sometimes they don't fit where you need them to go. Bow saws can also be kind of clumsy. The tool of choice for quickly shortening a branch is a lopper, a long-handled shear that makes short work of branches on the tree or off. When you move the handles together, the leverage created by the long handles moves the blade past the jaw, and the action neatly severs the branch. The cutting action is aided by the blade's curved edge. Assuming the blade is sharp and free of sticky sap, rust, or dirt, you'll get a nice clean cut and the tree or shrub will heal quickly.

Most loppers are single-action tools that chop through a branch in a single pass. But there are stronger ratchet models that close down on a branch and sever through it in stages.

ASK ROY

Q The ivy on our house and chimney is causing damage but it's pretty. Does it need to go?

A Ivy belongs on the ground, not on your house. The roots can be very damaging to brick, getting into and expanding any cracks in the mortar. Ivy holds in moisture, lifts gutters, and can creep into windows. It will also lift siding, which, along with being unsightly, provides an entrance for insects and mice into the house wall. As much as it might hurt, here's what you need to do: After using loppers and bypass shears to cut the ivy at ground level and everywhere else it's growing, pull it off the chimney as gently as possible. This leaves behind dozens of little suction cups known as holdfasts. Let them dry, and scrape them off with a putty knife. Remove remaining residue with a low-pressure power wash or by hand-scrubbing.

PICK AXE

A pick is like a pipe wrench—not very versatile, but when you need it, nothing else works nearly as well. If you spend most of your time breaking up hard, rocky soil, get a railroad pick—the type with either two pointed ends or a narrow chisel tip on one side and a pick on the other. Although using a railroad pick to break soft and medium-hard rock has become a dying art, it can be done if there's a crack in the rock where you can drive in the tip of the pick.

The tool can also be used for chopping through asphalt, and it's effective at severing small roots when equipped with a pick blade on one end and a mattock on the other. The mattock is the wide curved side, and, like any digging tool, if it's dinged or the metal appears dull, break out that file and hone the edge. You'll be glad you did.

TIP!

HOW TO CHOOSE A GOOD PICK AXE
When it comes time to buy your pick axe, select one with a drop-forged head. The head is balanced with the opposing pick or mattock and usually weighs 5 to 6 pounds. A pick isn't very heavy, but what makes it so effective is momentum. The weight of the swiftly swung head combined with a compact striking surface makes it an extremely effective digging tool. The angle of the head aids in both digging and prying, but it isn't the only thing providing leverage: a strong 36-inch handle made of hickory or fiberglass is instrumental in this tool's overall strength.

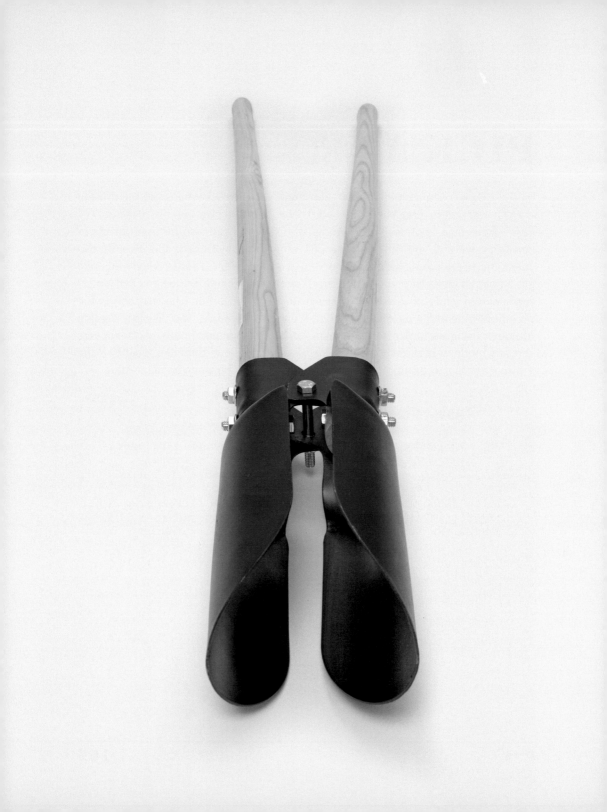

POST-HOLE DIGGER

No matter how you look at it, using a post-hole digger is serious work. Squeeze the handles together, drive it into the ground, separate the handles so the scoops grab up some dirt, lift up to remove dirt from the growing hole, and repeat. It's a tough slog, especially if the ground is hard.

When you're digging in hard soil or clay, loosen the dirt with a good-size digging bar. Once you've got a good amount loosened, use the post-hole digger to remove the loosened soil. To get around roots or rocks, rotate the blades so you can get past the interference. When digging a post hole, it's best to start with a narrow hole and dig wider as you get deeper. This will make a more stable footing for your posts.

Extremely loose or dry soil is another challenge. The soil needs to be moist, otherwise you won't be able to remove it with a post-hole digger, as the clamping action of the jaws is not effective on these materials. You must be able to compact the soil you're removing.

A dull cutting edge will make this job tougher than it has to be, so you might want to run a file over the cutting edges before a job, tuning them up just a bit.

For making a couple of holes, this tool is very useful. But if you've got a long fencing project or a deck with a dozen footings to dig, forgo this tool and head off to your local rental center to rent an auger. You'll be happy you did.

WISH LIST

SEYMOUR S500 INDUSTRIAL HERCULES POST-HOLE DIGGER
This classic Seymour product, built with 11-gauge hardened steel blades bolted to straight American Ash handles will last you a while. Yeah, it's a $150 hand tool, but then again, if you never have to replace it, you come out ahead.

PRUNER

pruner is a handheld version of a lopper. It's a tool that looks somewhat like a pair of pliers. But instead of just gripping something, it cuts. Many pruners have a spring-loaded handle that spreads apart the jaw and blade automatically. Slip the jaw and shear over the branch and close down on the handles to snip it.

There are two types of pruners. The most common one is a bypass type. Its design has the shear (or blade, if you prefer) that moves past the lower jaw. This is the tool for live pruning of shrubs or light work on trees. The other type is known as an anvil pruner. This type has a shear that closes down onto a lower jaw of plastic or brass. It's most widely used in cutting off dead wood, since the wood is dry and difficult to cut and doesn't lend itself to a neat bypass shearing action.

Pruners come in many shapes and sizes. There are small, delicate scissor types of pruners with two blades that are used for working on delicate flowering plants, small topiary, and bonsai plants. Most serious gardeners own a variety of pruners. For the rest of us, who simply dabble, a single high-quality bypass pruner is all we need. Keep it clean and sharp and you're good to go.

TIP!

HOW TO TRIM A TREE

Trees often develop a codominant stem that competes with the main one. If the errant stem isn't removed, the tree will have a weakened multi-forked trunk. Wind blowing over crossing branches will cause the two branches to rub together, damaging their bark. Prune away one or both crossing branches. Remove upward- and downward-pointing branches that emerge from an otherwise healthy lateral branch. These oddly angled branches are trouble for the lateral branch, liable to weaken, not strengthen it. Trim a broken branch as soon as possible to produce a clean stub and to reduce the chance of fungal infection entering through a ragged break. Suckers, small perpendicular branch-like shoots that come out of the tree's trunk, make it look unattractive and are prone to breaking. Prune them close to the trunk.

ROPE

Rope can be used for so many things: to hold objects in place, to lift things, to tow them. Or you can use it to make a kid's swing or create safety lines when people work up high. So it's important to choose a rope that has the strength and durability for your specific job.

For general use, not safety or climbing, a few things to consider are a rope's minimum breaking strength (a theoretical value) and its minimum working load limit, a more realistic number that helps you determine if the rope is suited for the job. One or both may be included on the rope's packaging. To be more precise, see the handy guide produced by the Cordage Institute that helps you determine how to safely use rope.

Natural fiber rope is great for general use, but for outdoor use, look for one that's specially treated for water. Natural fibers tend to swell when wet and stiffen once they dry. They are also susceptible to rotting. Polyester ropes are ideal for most outdoor applications.

Cutting rope isn't hard, but there's a trick to keep the ends from unraveling. Simply wrap the area you want to cut with a durable tape—duct tape comes to mind—and then cut with a sharp knife. The tape will keep the ends from coming undone.

For climbing, caving, or as safety lines, kernmantle rope is unsurpassed. Besides knotting easily, it's dynamic. If you happen to fall, a kernmantle rope will stretch to gradually absorb the impact. The rate of stretch is about 10 percent, or 5 feet of stretch for every 50 feet of rope. The reason for this built-in braking system is that it lessens the jolt a climber or roofer will suffer from a sudden stop if they happen to fall.

ROUND NOSE SHOVEL

The round nose shovel digs, cuts, and pries, but like any tool, its efficiency depends on you. Start with the shovel perpendicular to the soil and use your weight and leg muscles, not your arms, to drive it down. To toss dirt, hold the shovel close and keep your forward hand on the blade socket. Bend both knees. If you're right-handed, point your left foot in the direction of the toss.

Because you'll be placing your foot on what's called the shovel's shoulder (the flat part of the head perpendicular to the handle), we suggest looking for a shovel with a wider shoulder, to distribute the digging force. Try to use your heel and not the arch of your foot.

Buy a good-quality shovel and it will last you a long time. Look for one with a stainless-steel blade, but in a pinch, alloy steel will last reasonably well. No matter the length of the handle (see below) you'll need to select a strong hardwood, such as ash or hickory, or a reinforced fiberglass shaft. The handle should be riveted with metal plates on its cross-piece. Make sure the hollow shaft socket and blade are forged in one piece.

TIP!

GET BOTH TYPES OF HANDLES
There's more than just one version of this irreplaceable tool. We suggest stocking two versions of it: a longer handle and the shorter D-handle. A longer handle will give you more leverage for tasks like prying out a stubborn root or a good-size stone, and the short D-handled shovel is terrific where space is at a premium.

SQUARE NOSE SHOVEL

With a squared, flat, even edge, this is not a digging tool. It's for leveling areas for patios or walkways, squaring ditches, and clearing gravel, sand, or snow from surfaces. Its square-headed design makes it ideal for scooping debris and measuring material. When using it to place concrete, work the back of the blade against the inside surface of a slab form to consolidate concrete there.

Here's a great back-saving technique when creating a flat-bottomed hole with your shovel. Simply place the back face of a square-nosed shovel flat against the earth, so that the butt of the handle hits around your hips. Keep your spine straight as you walk the shovel forward, plowing forward with your leg muscles while the shovel collects the loose dirt like a dustpan.

Leveling ground isn't all this tool is good for: It can also strip roofing shingles. The flat head lets you get under roofing nails, and the leverage of the handle makes popping them out a real breeze. When removing shingles, it's best to start from the ridge and proceed down. It's also handy for remodelers, since it acts as a virtual plaster plow when run horizontally against a wall along the lathe. The long, flat blade is also handy for popping drywall off walls during demolition.

TIP!

HOW TO REPLACE A SHOVEL HANDLE
This is one of those disappearing rural skills that demonstrates basic mechanical competence. The most overlooked part of the job is getting the grain direction right. First, cut or grind off the rivets and slide the old handle out of the blade socket. When you mount the new handle, orient its grain so that the oval rings are to the side of the handle, not on the top or bottom [relative to the blade].

WHEELBARROW

No other gardening device has been the subject of such intense observation and improvement over such a long period of time as the humble wheelbarrow or its cousin, the garden cart. Both trace their origins to the dawn of wheeled transport, and no less a mechanical authority than Thomas Jefferson made notes, comments, and sketches regarding their design.

Modern wheelbarrows and carts come in almost every shape, size, and material—not to mention price. The differences between carts and wheelbarrows is slight, so much so that many products today blur the line between the two. For one thing, a wheelbarrow has one or two wheels, but a cart is always a two-wheeled affair. Generally, a wheelbarrow has its wheels in front of its tray. The front wheel position (especially when it is a single wheel) gives a wheelbarrow somewhat more maneuverability than a cart and allows you to dump its contents easily. A cart, on the other hand, usually has more capacity and is more stable while being moved or loaded.

There are times when you need the toughest product you can lay your hands on. For those times, this is the wheelbarrow for you. Called the C6, it's a contractor-grade wheelbarrow that consists of a 6-cubic-foot tray supported at the front with a pair of heavy uprights. A raised rim around each tray bolt prevents the edge of a shovel or mortar hoe from catching on them. The tray has a heavy, well-rounded rim and a tough, electrostatically applied paint job. The undercarriage is an assembly that locks together with hook-shaped joints and large bolts. The ash handles are lacquered for weather resistance, and the wheel bearing is oil-impregnated for maximum durability.

PROJECT

How to Build a Bluestone Patio

oncrete patios are functional. But they're not beautiful. Bluestone patios are both. A bluestone patio provides a place to grill and to host the dinner parties that some people insist they get pleasure out of throwing. It's always a perfect place to fall asleep on Saturday mornings, when it's too late to be in bed but too early for college football. For you, it may be a place for sunrise breakfasts or a kiddie pool or the perfect spot to set up that bistro table you saw on Pinterest. However you plan on using a patio, you need to choose the right material to build it. Concrete is durable and long-lasting, and brick is attractive, but the best option we've found is bluestone. These multihued slabs are the perfect pavement. They have a delicate and subtle color that weathers nicely, and they never crack. One downside is that bluestone is not easy to work with. It's heavy, at approximately 159 pounds per cubic foot. But the results are worth it.

Instructions

1. Choose the dimensions for your patio, then mark them off by driving batter boards (H-shaped stakes) a couple feet outside the corners of the four boundaries. You want them far enough away from the perimeter that you won't need to move anything during construction. Stretch mason's string between the stakes to mark the edges of the patio. Clip a line level to the mason's string to ensure an accurate horizontal reference.

Continued →

(2) Use a square-nose shovel to create the perimeter of your hole. Cut the hole 8 inches deep—enough to accommodate the layers of support beneath the stones and the stones themselves. The sides should be clean and square. Check the bottom of the hole for level with a 4-foot level. If you don't have one, you can place a smaller level on top of a long straight piece of lumber to get the same effect. Backfill any areas that were cut too deep and use a hand tamper to firmly pack them. It's very important that each layer of your patio be level. Any shallow spots can cause water to pool, which creates puddles or, in the winter, ice patches.

(3) The next step is to add base material, usually crushed stone or gravel. Unlike soil, stone has a uniform hardness and provides efficient drainage. But before you can add that, you need to set up your screeds—straight pieces of lumber set parallel in the hole—about three feet apart. Two by fours positioned on edge work well. Sight down each to make sure that the boards are straight and do not crown, or rise up, in the middle, then check them for level in the hole. If your screeds aren't long enough to span the patio space, or if you don't have enough to cover the entire area at once, work in segments. Set your screeds in the

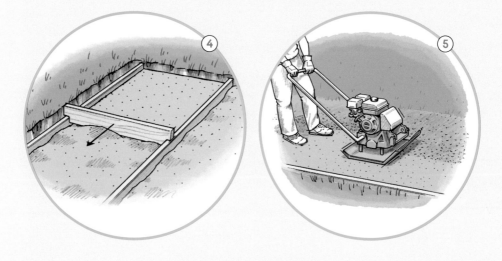

footprint of your patio. Hold them in place by packing base material around their sides, then dump 1 to 2 inches of base layer between the screeds. (Each layer is called a lift.) Distribute the stone with a base rake, a wide aluminum plate with one smooth and one serrated edge. An ordinary bow rake will also work, but you'll need to rake several passes with the tines down, then flip the rake on its back for a few more passes.

④ Cut a piece of lumber to fit from one screed to the other, notching it, if necessary, to fit between them. This is called a screed board. Slide it over the material to level its surface.

⑤ Each lift needs to be compacted before the next is laid. After adding the first layer, remove the screeds and fill in the slots left behind with base material. Using a vibratory plate compactor, which you can rent at most hardware stores, start on the outside of your patio footprint and make a single lap around the perimeter. Then move in toward the center in concentric rings, overlapping each pass by half the width of the compactor's baseplate. One round of this should be enough. You'll know it's properly compacted if you can step on the

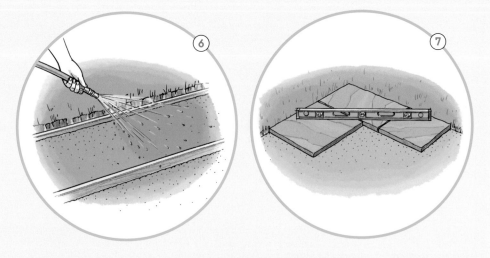

material and it doesn't take a footprint. Reset your screeds and add another 1- to 2-inch layer of base material. Remove the screeds, fill the remaining gaps, and compact again.

(6) The next lift is the bedding layer, which can be anything from finer crushed stone to sand. This layer provides a softer surface for the bluestones to settle into. Place your screeds over the base layer, then add 1 to 2 inches of bedding. After you've screeded the bedding layer, mist it with a fine spray from a garden hose. The water lubricates the stone or sand particles in the bedding and allows a firmer pack. Remove the screeds, fill the leftover slots, and compact the bedding layer.

(7) Start at one corner and run the first row of stones on the bedding, as close to each other as possible. Given that the face of the stone against the bedding is relatively uneven and the stone's thickness varies, to avoid wobbles you'll need to level each one by making slight adjustments to the bedding material. Use a concrete float to smooth the bedding material after making those adjustments, and tap each stone level with a dead-blow mallet. An easy way to check for level is to lower your string line so it sits a little bit above

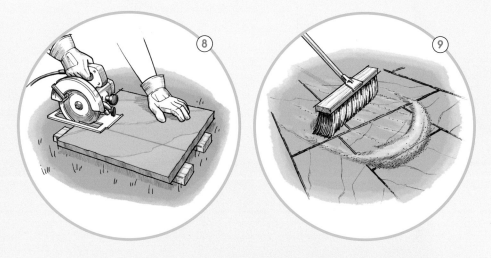

the stones—the thickness of a scrap of lumber. Now you can slide the lumber across the stones, and if it fits perfectly between the line and the stone, you know your patio is level.

8. If you need to cut any stones for fit, do it with a circular saw and a diamond-grit masonry blade. If you find yourself doing a lot of cutting, you can always rent a gas engine power cutter. Whichever method you choose, use a spray bottle to mist water on the blade to reduce dust.

9. Use a large exterior broom to sweep bedding material over the surface of the patio to fill in the joints. After the surface has been thoroughly swept in, mist it with a garden hose to consolidate the material. A garden edger is a useful tool for packing the material between joints. It's just the right width and lets you remain standing as you pack. Repeat the process until the joints are completely filled and packed.

MECHANICAL

Adjustable Wrench............177
Air Compressor..................179
Allen Wrench.....................181
Angle Grinder....................183
Ball-Peen Hammer.............185
Center Punch.....................187
Cold Chisel.......................189
Combination Wrench..........191
Cup Plunger......................193
Die...................................195
Drill Bits..........................197
Fish Tape..........................199
Hacksaw...........................201
Machinist Vise..................203
Metal File.........................205

Multibit Screwdriver.......207
Needle-Nose Pliers..........209
Pipe and Tubing
Cutter..............................211
Pipe Wrench.....................213
Plumber's Snake...............215
Side-Cutting Pliers..........217
Socket Wrench..................219
Soldering Torch................221
Tap..................................223
Tongue and Groove
Pliers...............................225
Vise-Grip.........................227
Volt/Ohm Meter................229
Wire Stripper....................231

ADJUSTABLE WRENCH

Solymon Merrick is credited with the patent on the adjustable wrench in 1835, and as the tool's name implies, it can fit a variety of sized nuts or bolts. The jaw opens by turning a wheel at the head and is good for imperial as well as metric-size fasteners. If you're going to own just one, make it a 10- or 14-inch model so that it's big enough for residential plumbing fittings. They do range in size from the ultra-portable 4-inch, which is great for cyclists making roadside bike repairs, to the industrial-size 24-inch.

Whether you're tightening or loosening a fastener, be sure the fixed jaw, not the moveable part, is applying the force. Position yourself so you are pulling the wrench, not pushing it. Pushing it raises the risk of the wrench slipping. If you do apply force to the moveable jaw, there's a chance that it might move and slip off the bolt, possibly banging up your knuckles and rounding the edges of your fastener, which will make it very difficult to tighten or loosen it further.

Many mechanics will recommend using an adjustable wrench only for plumbing. There's too much movement in the jaws, often called slop, which creates a knuckle-buster waiting to happen, and they would recommend a good set of fixed wrenches instead. But for a quick job, or just to lighten your toolbox, an adjustable wrench is just the right tool most of the time.

TIP!

KEEP YOUR WRENCH USE PAIN-FREE

Crescent wrenches have a propensity to slip off of nuts, which can lead to injury. To do it right: First, pull the wrench, don't push it. Second, make sure the fixed jaw is applying the force—the adjustable jaw can come loose under pressure. This means putting the fixed jaw on the far side of the nut from your body and pulling the wrench handle in the clockwise direction.

AIR COMPRESSOR

More than a tool for inflating tires, an air compressor is an invaluable alternate power source for your shop.

Years ago, it was common for shops to have a central power source that drove all the tools through a system of belts, wheels, and driveshafts. The power was routed around the work space by mechanical means. While the belts and shafts may be gone, many shops still use a mechanical system to move power around the shop. It's based on the energy stored in air under pressure, and the heart of the system is the air compressor.

You'll find air compressors used in a wide range of situations—from corner gas stations to major manufacturing plants. And, more and more, air compressors are finding their way into home workshops, basements, and garages. Models sized to handle every job, from inflating pool toys to powering tools such as nail guns, sanders, drills, impact wrenches, staplers, and spray guns are now available through local home centers, tool dealers, and mail-order catalogs.

The big advantage of air power is that each tool doesn't need its own bulky motor. Instead, a single motor on the compressor converts the electrical energy into kinetic energy. This makes for light, compact, easy-to-handle tools that run quietly and have fewer parts that wear out. When choosing a compressor, make sure it can supply the amount of air and the pressure that your tools need. Check the cfm (cubic feed per minute) and psi (pounds per square inch) ratings.

ALLEN WRENCH

Also known as hex wrenches or hex keys, Allen wrenches have a hexagonal cross section to fit screwheads with hexagonal recesses, common in bicycles, motorcycle engines, and, increasingly, build-it-yourself furniture. With motorcycles, Allen fastener heads allow an engine cover to be mounted flush to an engine case without protruding bolt heads. Unlike the Phillips heads briefly used in mid-'80s Japanese bikes, the Allen bolts can actually be removed—as long as you have the right size for the job.

Allen wrenches are made in fractional inch and metric sizes. The three most common sizes are $5/32$-inch, $3/16$-inch, and $1/4$-inch; in metric, 4, 5, and 6 millimeters. Other good imperial sizes to own are $3/32$-inch, $7/64$-inch, $1/8$-inch, $9/64$-inch, and $1/32$-inch. It's difficult to say what sizes are common when assembling furniture, because as anyone with experience at that job knows, those little L-shaped keys tend to disappear immediately.

This is why storage is critical. Keeping the tools together on a ring is a good start. But as long as you're working with an L-shaped tool shorter than a broken pencil, you're always going to have a little stub of metal gouging your palm with each turn. The best bet is to find a tool with some thought put into its design.

Some options include the convenient, traditional fold-up style, in which the wrenches pull out like pocketknives from a nicely sized handle; or the more unusual three-way wrenches, which arrange common sizes on an easy-to-grip disk shaped like a Chinese throwing star. If you really want to get fancy (and save serious time and effort), consider investing in Garrett Wade's ratcheting Allen wrench.

ANGLE GRINDER

Good for grinding metal, this often-overlooked tool has a myriad of uses. It is great at cutting, polishing, or filing metal. For hardscaping projects like cutting brick or bluestone, simply install a diamond wheel and you can make some intricate designs and patterns out of stone. Angle grinders are also handy tile tools. They don't just cut tile; you can use them to make repairs in an existing tile field.

We're just getting started with things you can do with these tools. This machine will let you put an edge on a lawnmower blade that's tackled a few too many stones. If your round nose shovel just isn't cutting the turf, it's a quick fix with this machine. Hoes, picks, and any garden implement with a blunted edge can get a quick tune-up from an angle grinder.

Rusty metal, flaking paint, crumbled mortar, or spalled concrete: the grinder has a wheel to deal with these obstacles. If you need to cut an old bolt, a hacksaw might take a while, but with an angle grinder, it'll take just a few seconds.

When buying an angle grinder, look for a tool that will pull 5 amps or better. With power tools, more amps equals more power. Many of these tools have a switch at the head. This can be a bit cumbersome, and we think a paddle switch that runs the length of the tool, like a long trigger, offers more control. The paddle also works as a great kill switch, if you ever drop the tool. It just shuts down, and that's a great safety measure. As with using any tool turning at nearly 10,000 rpm and shooting a rooster tail of bright orange sparks, wearing a pair of heavy-duty leather gloves and eye protection is an absolute must.

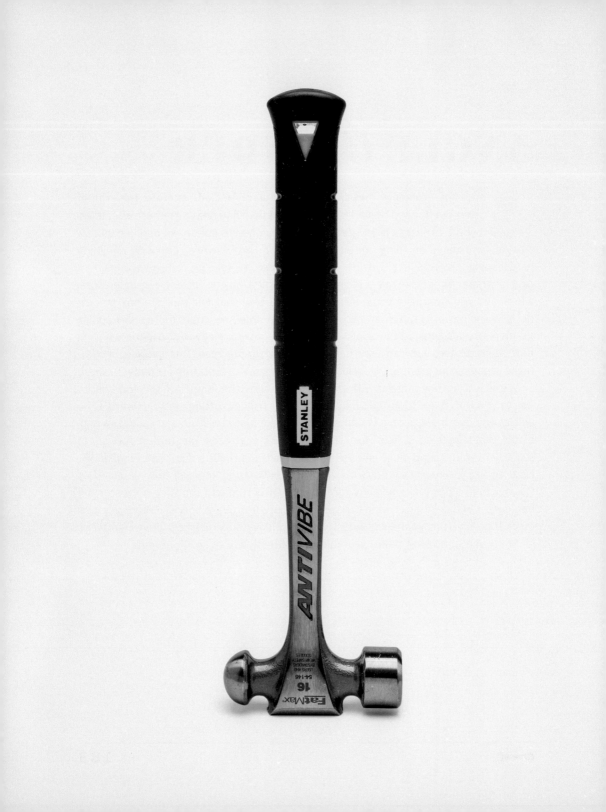

BALL-PEEN HAMMER

The face of a ball-peen hammer strikes cold chisels and punches, while the dome-shaped end rolls over the edges of rivets (peening) or works curved sheet metal. The hammer ranges in size from 4 to 50 ounces (with large models serving as blacksmiths' hammers), but the 16-ounce size works well and fits in a crowded toolbox.

A ball-peen (or ball-pein) won't chip when used against metal tools, unlike a carpenter's claw hammer, which is designed to strike relatively soft metal (namely, a nail). The tool is ideal for shaping metal, and the peen end is ideally suited for thinning metal when you want the metal to move out in all directions.

When fixing a damaged body panel on a car, the ball-peen hammer's shape lets you tap out dents to reshape and repair the damage. Match the head size as closely as you can to the dent. Using a solid scrap of metal as a dolly on the top of the dent, you can tap the dent from behind and shape the repair. It does take some experience and finesse to work on your car, and gentle taps go a long way.

TIP!

HARD FACE VS. SOFT FACE
Don't expect to be shaping metal often? Look for a hard-face hammer in a light weight [8 to 12 ounces]. You'll use this versatile tool often when chiseling or working with metal sheets. But if you'll be working with soft metals like bronze or copper, you need a soft-face ball-peen, made of brass, plastic, or lead. Unfortunately, soft-face hammers will wear out over time, so be prepared to replace the head.

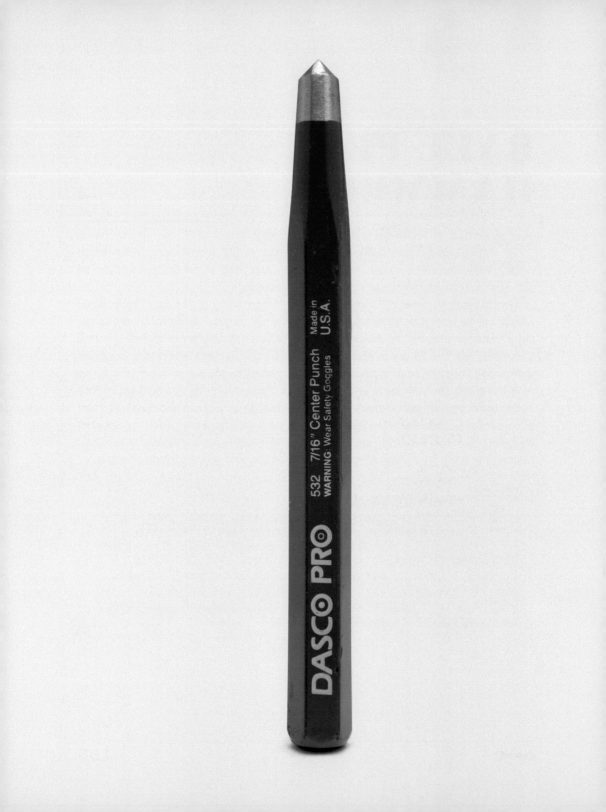

CENTER PUNCH

n theory, you use a center punch to start holes in metal. In practice, it's far more useful than that. You can tighten a loose handle on a knife or shovel by centering the punch on the rivet and then firmly striking it with a ball-peen hammer, expanding the rivet's head. In a pinch, you can also use a center punch to mark a line on wood or metal like a steel pencil, to countersink a large nail head, or to drive down the stub of a broken nail or staple.

While the old-school tool required some finesse, today's spring-loaded center punches take the hammer swing out of the equation (and save your bruised knuckles). Adjust the tension cap on the punch to the type of material you're working with and place the center punch onto your marked workpiece. The punch works just like clicking a pen.

A punch also gives your drill bit a head start when working with metal or dense woods. The precise indentation gives some initial bite and lowers the risk of having your drill bit move across and mar the surface of your workpiece. A spring-loaded center punch is ideal for starting screw holes for things like hinges, hasps, and drawer pulls.

TIP!

HOW TO USE A PUNCH
To use this handy tool, you will set its point on dead center and strike the punch with a hammer. If the mark is not accurate, angle the punch toward the true center, tap it to extend the mark in that direction, and then mark the center again.

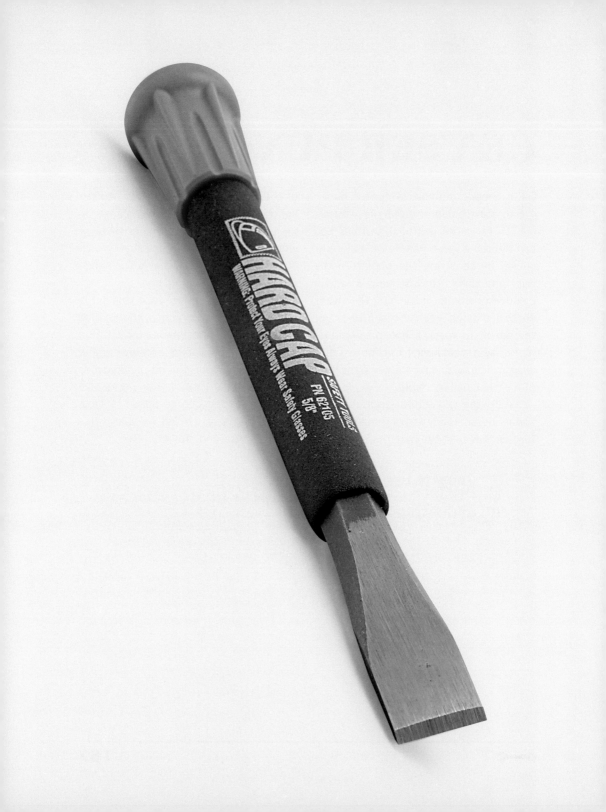

COLD CHISEL

Use a cold chisel to chop through bolts, rivets, and pins, and to cut cold (as opposed to torch- or forge-heated) metal. Strike it with a ball-peen hammer, preferably one with a head ⅛-inch larger than the end of the chisel. You can get a better view of the tip by gripping the body with tongue-and-groove pliers. Always wear safety glasses when striking a cold chisel, and never use it on stone or concrete.

Some of these tools are now equipped with polymer caps, which does two things. First, it reduces the "mushrooming head" and the risk of flying metal fragments during impact. Second, the polymer cap forms a larger striking surface than the chisel itself, and that protects your hand as you hold the chisel.

A cold chisel is generally used to remove waste metal when a smooth finish isn't required. Because these tools are used to cut metal, they have a less acute cutting angle than a typical wood chisel. This gives the tool a less sharp, but stronger, cutting edge.

TIP!

HOW MANY CHISELS DO YOU NEED?
While the flat chisel is a must for your toolbox, you may need a variety of sizes on standby for different projects. We recommend picking up a three- or five-piece set containing a mix of sizes, including a ¼-inch and a ¾-inch. And one more tip: We suggest slipping a plastic safety sleeve over the chisel to protect your hand from a misplaced blow with a hammer. Some chisels, such as STANLEY's FATMAX series, come with this installed.

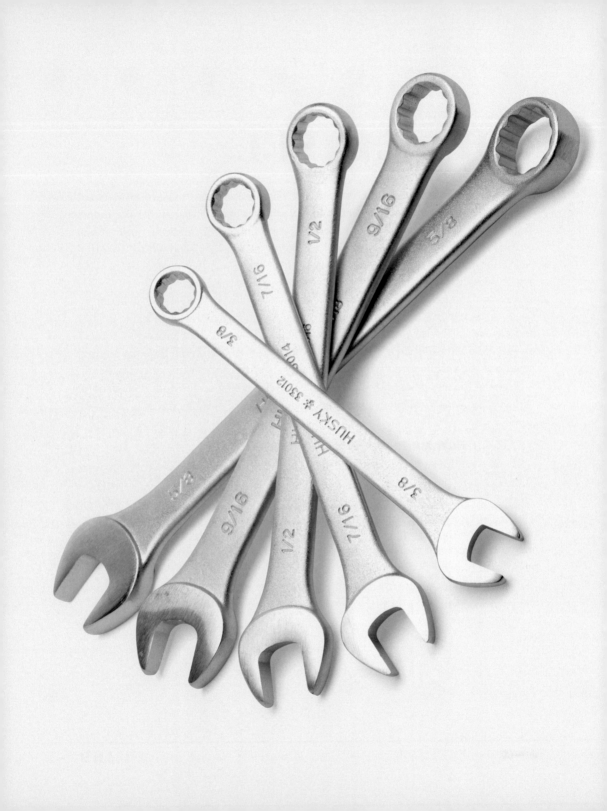

COMBINATION WRENCH

You'll find that your set of combination wrenches will become one of your most cherished possessions. The tool's design is prototypically simple—box-end on one side, open on the other. It has no moving parts and is covered in shiny chrome. If you're lucky enough to have inherited the set from a parent, then it's filled with memories, too.

No one knows who invented the combination wrench or when, but it was popularized in the United States by Plomb Tools in the 1930s, a period of social and technological ferment. As automobiles became more numerous and sophisticated, so did the tools to work on them. New steel alloys and forging methods have only improved the wrench with the passage of time.

Today's wrench is thinner, sleeker, and stronger than the bulky ones it replaces; it weighs half what it did in the '20s. While it is hard to improve on perfection, in 2006 Craftsman introduced a new twist—literally—in its Cross Force combination wrenches, turning the handle so your palm presses on the tool's broad face, not the narrow edge.

You can purchase sets in a variety of assortments, but whatever set you purchase should include at least these seven sizes: $3/8$-, $7/16$-, $1/2$-, $9/16$-, $5/8$-, $11/16$-, and $3/4$-inch. And if you'll be working on anything outside the U.S., add five metric wrenches to your set, too, ranging from 10mm to 14mm.

Back when blacksmiths forged tools, they would inscribe the year on the head, as if to announce that it would last decades, maybe centuries, into an uncertain future. A fine set of wrenches, bearing dates or not, exudes the same sense of permanence.

CUP PLUNGER

This might be the first tool you should buy when you move into a home. Plugged sinks are gross. Plugged toilets even more so. You just want to get rid of the clog and move on with your day. You need a plunger. More specifically, it's called a cup plunger. Cupped over a drain hole or toilet outlet, it creates a powerful push-pull action that flushes clogs out of the trap and drain pipe. When followed by a flush of clean water, you'll be moving on with the rest of your day in no time.

There are several types of this indispensable tool. The first is a simple cup-shaped variety. It fits most sink and tub drains and some older toilet styles, though it's not particularly effective on newer toilets. The next type is called a force plunger, and it has an extended cup that folds out over a smaller inner ring. The fold-out design of the cup allows it to fit sinks, tubs, and many toilet outlets. A variation on this type of plunger is the bellows style. It consists of an extended cup backed by a bellows. Manufacturers say that it produces more flushing force than a standard cup plunger. Our tests show that they're no more effective than traditional designs.

A newer beehive-shaped plunger is designed specifically for toilets, especially the new so-called high-efficiency toilets with a keyhole-shaped outlet. The tool's T handle enables a really powerful grip and an effective downward push to blast out blockages.

TIP!

WHY YOU NEVER BUY A SMALL PLUNGER
The important consideration is the depth of the cup. Because plungers push and pull air and water to break clogs, the greater the volume of air in the cup, the greater the force. On plungers with a collapsible funnel, when the funnel is folded in, it can be used on standard basin fixtures. When extended, it has the power to clear partially clogged toilets. Avoid smaller plungers. While they're easy to store, you'll get little clog-busting force.

DIE

For everything that goes wrong with a tapped hole, the same thing happens to the fastener that threads into it. And so for every tap, there's a matching die. Bolts, machine screws, studs, and pipe all rust, or their threads strip, dull, or become clogged.

Fortunately, a die rescues them from becoming scrap metal. This donut-shaped piece of tool steel is inserted in a two-handle device called a die stock. Fitted over the bar (pipe, fastener, screw, or fitting) and turned firmly with two hands, the die carves an exterior thread.

ASK ROY

Ⓠ **The threaded steel pipe in the basement leaks. My husband has taken it apart, wrapped it with tape, and put it back together. Twice. It still leaks. Can you help?**

Ⓐ When a threaded joint leaks, the natural response is to tighten it. Sometimes that stops the drip, but if you overtighten the joint, you could ruin the threaded parts and make the problem worse. Most likely only one of the pipe's fittings has stripped threads. To fix it, replace the pipe and bad fitting. There's no need to replace the fitting at the other end. First, apply a generous amount of professional-grade pipe sealant such as RectorSeal No. 5 to the male threads of the new pieces. Once the new pieces are as snug as you can get them with your bare hands, you need only a full turn to a turn and a half with tools. Hold the fitting or the pipe with one wrench, and with another turn the part you are tightening. Plumbers call this back holding. With RectorSeal you can send water through immediately.

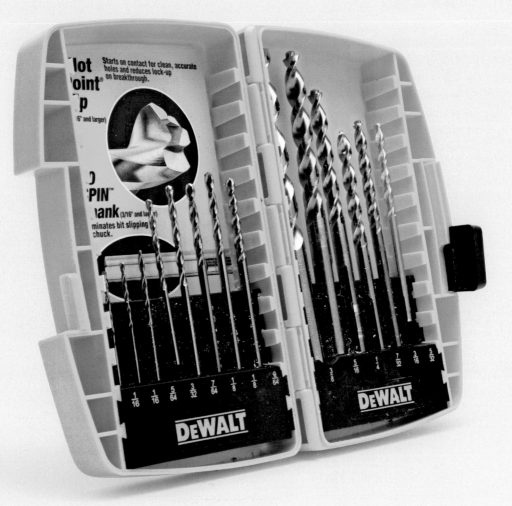

DRILL BITS

For general hole drilling, a set of fifteen or eighteen high-speed steel twist drill bits will suffice. These bits work great on wood and most plastics.

Titanium nitride–coated bits are a better choice for industrial use or drilling truly abrasive materials, like cast iron. The titanium nitride coating over the high-speed steel improves the bit's abrasion resistance, helping it hold an edge longer. Expensive specialty bits like concrete bits, auger bits, and countersinks come in handy as well. We suggest buying these bits individually, as the need arises, instead of an entire set.

It's important to make sure you're using the right bit. Spade bits cut aggressively and are designed for quick, rough holes. Screw-point auger bits pull themselves through the wood and bore with high speed, leaving a relatively rough exit hole. Hollow-center auger bits are aggressive enough to cut right through nails and will chug through green, wet wood. Brad-point twist bits bore with high speed and precision, leaving a clean exit hole. Finally, Forstner bits cut large diameter holes (up to 4 inches across). These larger-diameter bits are intended to be used in a drill press.

TIP!

DON'T THROW OLD BITS AWAY. SHARPEN THEM.
Heat and friction rob our bits of a honed edge, just as dropping them or hitting a nail will. But don't toss your dull bits; sharpen them using a Drill Doctor. This handy accessory will help you keep your bits sharper than on the day you bought them, and using it is as easy as sharpening a pencil. The budget model [DD350X] is great for hobbyists, but if you're looking to resurrect those custom, carbide-tipped masonry bits, you'll need the DD750X.

FISH TAPE

L et's say you're expanding the home office or stereo system in your existing home. The only way to get that wire or cable from Point A to Point B is to run it through the wall. But how do you get back there? With fish tape. You attach the wire or cable to a thin, flexible piece of spring steel and pull it from one place to another through the wall cavity—a process known as fishing. Not that it's easy. Often, these jobs will try every bit of patience you have.

To do this, you start by drilling a hole or making some sort of entrance (like removing a piece of trim) in a wall and then feed the tape into the cavity with the goal of it emerging through the other hole or access point you've made. If things go smoothly, the tape pops out at its intended location. You take your cable and very securely wind and tape it around the fish tape, then pull the tape and the cable up or down where it needs to go. But a lot of times you'll hit a pipe, an electrical cable, a sheet metal duct or a piece of wood inside the wall. At which point you curse, pull the tape back out, and try another entry point.

SHOP NOTES

WHEN THE FISH TAPE WON'T REACH

There are times when a length of conduit outstretches the fish tape. Then what? Tie some monofilament fishing line around a small sponge ball or a wadded-up plastic bag, then stuff it into one end of the conduit. Attach a shop vac to the other end and flick the switch. Within seconds, the sponge or bag is drawn through the conduit and into the vacuum. Now use the fishing line to pull the wires.

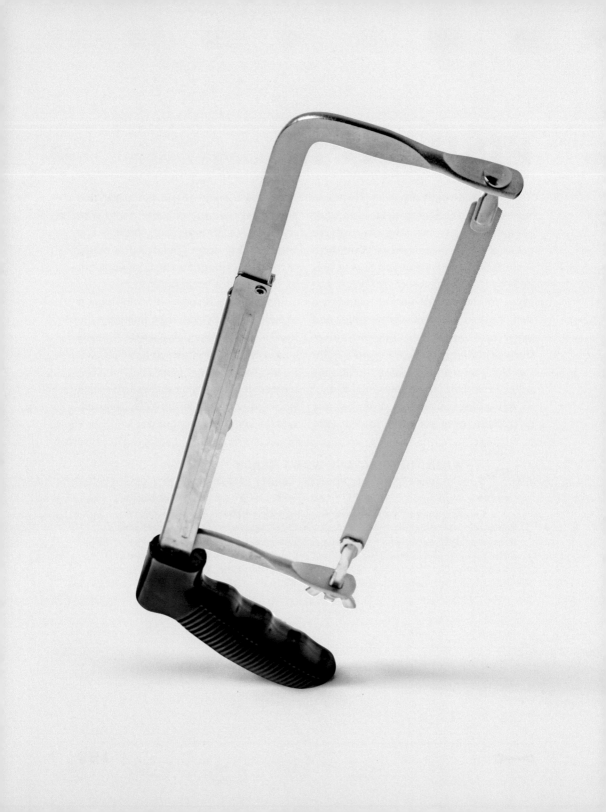

HACKSAW

The fine-tooth blade of a hacksaw can cut through iron and steel as well as through tough materials like hard plastics and cable. With a blade known as a carbide-grit rod saw, it can even slice through ceramic tile. For metal, use a carbon-steel blade with 14, 18, 24, or 32 teeth per inch. Opt for a bimetal blade for high-tension pro models, which exert tremendous tensile force to hold the blade arrow straight in tough cuts. The bimetal blade's carbon-steel back bonded to a high-speed-steel front can take the tension.

A hacksaw frame can be fixed or adjustable. An adjustable frame gives you some room to pick blades from 8 to 16 inches in length. In addition to the adjustable frames, the posts that hold the blades can be set in different positions, so you can cut left, right, up, or down.

When installing the blade, the teeth should be pointing forward, or away from the handle. Your cut time should be one second per stroke. Use the length of the blade when possible, so take it slow. Since you create a great deal of heat when using a hacksaw, a drop or two of clear cutting oil will help reduce the heat and keep your blade sharp for a longer time.

HOW TO HACK YOUR HACKSAW

TIP!

A hacksaw is perfect to saw off those large bolts, stuck screws, and broken hardware, but sometimes there's just no room to manuever. We suggest combining the best of two worlds: Grip a hacksaw blade in a pair of locking pliers. And for those really confined spaces, use a snapped-off piece of hacksaw blade.

MACHINIST VISE

Whether stationary or swiveling, a vise is like an extra set of (really strong) hands for securing your work. Cast-iron models function well for most applications, but buy a forged-steel vise for anything heavy-duty. If you cut a lot of pipe, choose a vise with V-shaped jaws to grip round material, but be careful not to overtighten the pipe. You'll knock it out of round. For moderate metal pounding, choose one with an anvil behind the jaws. While it's no substitute for a blacksmith anvil, it is handy for small projects.

When using a vise for wood projects, pad the jaws with wood scraps and don't overtighten the jaws. Otherwise, you run the risk of compressing the wood fibers, which can lead to cracking or splitting your workpiece.

A swiveling vise is a more versatile tool, since you move the tool to suit your needs and not the other way around. But a machinist vise doesn't have to stay in the shop, attached to a bench. Most plumbers and welders will have one attached to the bumper of their work truck, turning the truck bed into a veritable mobile workshop. They keep the vise from rusting with a liberal amount of WD-40, a wire brush, and a large plastic freezer bag as a cover.

WISH LIST

BUY THE BEST VISE
Our favorite heavy-duty vise has a 4-inch jaw spread and an anvil for whacking stuff into place: Irwin's 226304. Use it for everything from home welding and steel cutting to clamping bar stock. A swivel base is for optimum positioning; the built-in pipe clamp is tuned for working round stock.

METAL FILE

ake it in a cake and you've got a tool to cut jail bars, but put it into the hands of a craftsman and it's a veritable magic wand. With metal files, there are two basic cutting designs: the single-cut file and the double-cut file.

The teeth on a single-cut file are in rows and are the best choice for smoothing. Double-cut files have teeth in a diamond pattern and remove more material per pass, leaving a rougher surface in their wake. Both types come in a variety of tooth size—smaller teeth, which correlates to more tpi, will produce a smoother cut for a finer finish. The most common metal file is the bastard file, which has 26 tpi. This is a good all-around file since it's neither too rough nor too smooth. Smoothing files range in tooth count from 60 tpi to what's known as a dead smooth file, which has 100 tpi. Rougher-cut files like the second-cut file have 36 tpi, and coarse files have 16 tpi.

Files also come in a number of different shapes, but for most uses, a flat, double-cut bastard file is considered the go-to tool. A rat-tail, or round file, is the right choice for sharpening serrated-edge tools.

When using a metal file, grasp the handle with one hand and grasp the point, or head, of the file with the other hand. Place the middle face of the file on your workpiece, and with a little pressure at the point of the file, push it across the surface you're smoothing. Use as much of the file per stroke as you can, then lift the file and start again without making contact on the return stroke.

TIP!

PROPER FILING TECHNIQUE
Since it only cuts in one direction, don't rub your file on the workpiece. Those return strokes only serve to dull the tool. And keep a file card on hand; this inexpensive tool has short "bristles" of wire that clean waste from between file teeth.

MULTIBIT SCREWDRIVER

You're up on a ladder changing the paddles on your ceiling fan, and you realize whoever installed it used whatever screws they could find. No matter what type they were. Lucky for you, you've got a compact and versatile screwdriver in your back pocket. Now you don't have to make another trip up and down the ladder to rifle through your toolbox for just the right driver—it's all in the palm of your hand. That's certainly one advantage to having a multitasking tool.

Many multibit screwdrivers are armed with magnetized, interchangeable tips, which are handy when you want to get a screw started or don't want it to drop. They are also handy at fishing a screw out of a tight spot. But you need to be careful around delicate and magnetically sensitive electronics when using a magnetized tip.

Handy for a quick repair around the house, the real potential in this compact tool is when storage space is limited, like when camping, fishing, or cycling. This tool earns its keep because the screwdriver tip should match the head of whatever screw you're turning, and having so many options in a tight spot is a good thing.

CHOOSE THE RIGHT MULTIBIT SCREWDRIVER

TIP! Trying to decide which option is right for you? There are several special features you should look out for. Craftsman's Autoloading model, for example, introduces the ability to switch bits without touching them; the 7-in-1 Twist-a-Nut from Ideal Industries includes a wire-nut wrench on the base of the handle; and Klenk Tool's Select-A-Bit screwdriver [pictured] features extra-long 3-inch bits that store in its handle.

NEEDLE-NOSE PLIERS

When you need to fish a dropped screw out of a tight space or when working on electronics, there's nothing handier than a pair of needle-nose pliers. Their elegant shape is also perfect for fastening a wire to a switch or an outlet receptacle: grip the wire at the tip of the jaws and roll the pliers to produce a neat hook, then fasten the hook under the terminal screw. These pliers also serve in a pinch as a cutting tool for small gauge wire.

Like any tool, you can find a myriad of uses for needle-nose pliers. Because the nose of the pliers is long and thin and has a knurled or crosshatched tip, it's easy to hold a brad or finishing nail and hammer it without hurting your fingers. For hanging picture hooks or doing any such small operations, it's a great advantage to drive the nail while keeping your hands out of the way. If you're nailing small trim details, it helps to either predrill for the fastener at your workbench or dull its tip by whacking it once with a hammer.

TIP!

GET MORE PLIERS THAN YOU THINK YOU'LL NEED
So just how many of these little wonders should you have around? We recommend one for each hand, and at least one very small pair if anyone in your home does any crafts with beads or jewelry. In addition to the straight-nose version, pick up a pair of bent-nose pliers. You never know when you'll need them.

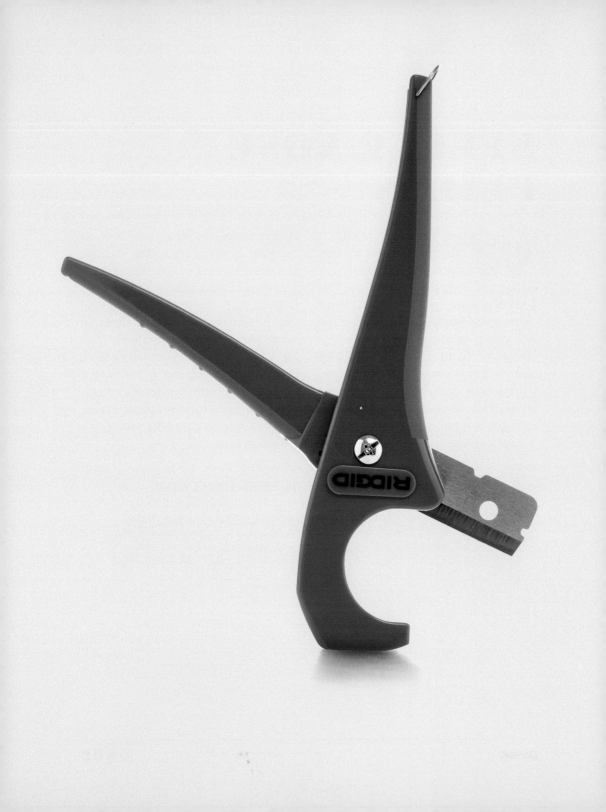

PIPE AND TUBING CUTTER

When it comes to running copper pipe for plumbing applications or copper tubing for gas lines—or any other thin-walled metal tube, whether it's brass, copper, aluminum, or conduit—a hacksaw should stay put. Reach for a better tool.

Tubing cutters are compact, require virtually no swing room, and can accommodate tubing with an outside diameter (OD) from ⅛-inch to 1⅛ inches. Simply set the tube into the jaws and turn the knurled knob that raises the cutting wheel until it's finger-tight. Once the cutting wheel has made contact, turn the tool a full turn around the tubing, scoring it. With each revolution, you'll raise the cutting wheel just a bit, and after two or three revolutions, the cut will be complete. The result is a super-clean perpendicular cut that provides the strongest, most secure joints when making soldered connections.

Ream off the small burr on the inside of the cut surface and you're ready to begin solder preparations for plumbing jobs or to fit up with conduit body and connectors for electrical work.

TIP!

MATCH YOUR TOOL TO THE JOB
Working with copper tubing or plastic? Or perhaps it's cast iron and concrete? Believe us when we say there's a cutter engineered specifically for every type of piping. For example, pictured is RIDGID's Scissor-Style Cutter, specifically created to swipe through all types of plastic and rubber tubing [up to 1¼ inch outside diameter] in one go-no ratcheting or twisting required. Copper and other metal pipes require a more recognizable design. Match your tool to the job for the cleanest cut: there's a tool developed for close quarters, soil pipes, and much more.

PIPE WRENCH

A pipe wrench may not be versatile, but when you need to hold a pipe and fittings, nothing else will work. The body is rigid and heavy, and the teeth bite forcefully into smooth, round surfaces. When working with delicate plumbing, wrap the pipe with a leather strap or some rags to prevent the wrench from damaging it. Though most pipe wrenches are cast iron, spring for a lighter aluminum model if you face a long day of plumbing.

Daniel Stillson, a steamboat firefighter, invented this useful tool and patented it in 1869. In fact, it was referred to as a Stillson wrench until its patent expired. When using a pipe wrench, keep the pressure on the hook jaw and turn it in the direction of the heel jaw. By using this movement, you ensure that the serrated jaws will bite into the workpiece and keep the wrench from slipping. While these serrated jaws are great for gripping, they are not very useful for tightening chrome-plated pipes or thin-walled copper tubing. Don't try.

Pipe wrenches aren't just for pipes. Their serrated teeth can bite into a stripped nut or bolt. Once the teeth bite in and you're turning in the right direction, the pipe wrench offers a lot of leverage to remove that smoothed-over fastener. But that's not all: don't tell any plumbers this, but this tool is great for demolition work, too. Hook that jaw around a nailed-down 2 x 4 and you'll show it who's boss.

HOW TO MAKE AN IMPROVISED PIPE WRENCH

SHOP NOTES

Improvise a pipe wrench with a length of rope and a metal bar, like a crowbar: When a pipe needs to be tightened, fold a rope in half and tie the ends together. Wrap the rope tightly around the pipe, tucking the tied end under one of the windings to hold it in place. Thread the metal bar through the loop at the other end of the rope. Twist the bar, and the rope tightens and twists the pipe.

PLUMBER'S SNAKE

When the old plunger just isn't cutting it, try a plumber's snake, sometimes called a hand auger, to unclog your drains. This hand-cranked drain-clearing tool has a long flexible steel cable that's extremely effective at clearing obstructions from tubs, showers, sinks, toilets, and drain lines.

Snakes come in a variety of sizes and lengths. For most people, a ⅜-inch-diameter, 20-foot-long snake is all you'll ever need. At the business end of the snake is a spring-shaped head wider than the snake itself. This "spring" engages the clog, and as the snake gets rotated and pulled and pushed, it breaks up the clog. Once the snake engages the clog, it will be more difficult to turn the snake. Push into the clog and pull back, but don't force the snake; there's a chance it can get stuck or snap off.

If it's a sink drain you're clearing, make sure there's some water in it. Not only will this provide some much needed lubrication, but also the water pressure along with the snake might send the clog exactly where you want it—down the drain and gone.

AVOID A PLUG IN THE FIRST PLACE

TIP!

If your kitchen drain clogs regularly, make sure your dishwashing habits are not contributing to the problem. The worst kitchen drain clogger is grease. We suggest pouring off grease from cookware into a container, then disposing of it when it has cooled. Also, remove and inspect the trap to confirm that hardened minerals or debris are not blocking it. Replace the trap if its internal diameter has been reduced by hardened buildup. And then it's time to take out your plumber's snake and thoroughly clear those pipes.

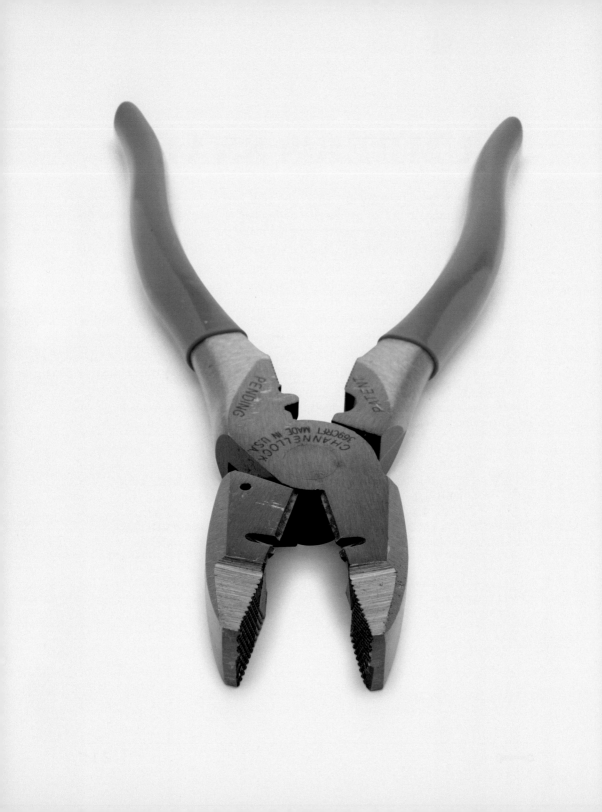

SIDE-CUTTING PLIERS

Call them side cutters, linesman pliers, or electrician's pliers. By any name, the heavy jaws and shears make this tool indispensable for cutting electrical cable and for pulling the steel tape used to fish wires through wall and ceiling cavities. Models rated as "high leverage" can cut nails and bolts, while those equipped with a die near the jaws can press together the crimp connectors used on grounding wires. It's a multifunctional tool with dexterity to boot.

When cutting with these tools, always make sure you, and anyone around you, are wearing safety glasses. You should never cut hardened wire unless the pliers are specifically engineered for this use. If the knives can't make the cut at a right angle, you need bigger pliers.

And it should go without saying that you should never work on live wires. Those plastic-dipped handles aren't insulated unless the manufacturer says they are specifically rated as so; that plastic coating is for comfort, not functionality.

 TIP!

KNOW YOUR CUTTING PLIERS
Linesman pliers share the name of side cutting pliers with diagonal pliers ["dikes" for short], which has only one function: cutting wire. Linesman pliers cut and grab, and some models [like the one pictured] also strip and crimp. All linesman pliers are side cutters, but not all side cutters are linesman pliers.

SOCKET WRENCH

R each for a socket wrench when you need to tighten nuts and bolts or loosen frozen ones. The ½-inch drive is the heavy hitter of the socket wrench kingdom, followed by a switch-hitter, the ⅜-inch drive, which is big enough to do light-duty automotive work yet small enough for some appliances. Reserve the ¼-inch drive for appliance and electronics repair.

A socket fully engages a bolt's head and equally distributes the torque, minimizing the chance of stripping it. With an extension, a socket can loosen or tighten a bolt in a narrow space, allowing you to engage the ratchet with maximum leverage. The prime advantage in using a socket wrench is speed. The ratcheting in the wrench allows you to loosen or tighten a nut or bolt without having to remove and refit the wrench with each turn.

What makes a socket wrench tick? Inside the bulbous end of the socket wrench is a gear with two step-levers, or pawls. The step-levers are responsible for which direction you turn the wrench. The lever mechanism catches into a groove and allows the wrench to lock, so you can apply force in one direction and let the wrench swing unhindered in the other. This is the heart of the tool, but it can also be its Achilles' heel. There's a lot of tension placed on these pawls during use, so you'll want them to be strong. Bargain-bin socket wrenches can spill their guts after just a few uses, and when you depend on your tools to get you through your workday, it pays to buy the best you can afford. If you're at a loss as to which brand to buy, call a mechanic. Most mechanics are willing to talk shop and give you some insight. Snap-on or Craftsman are a safe bet.

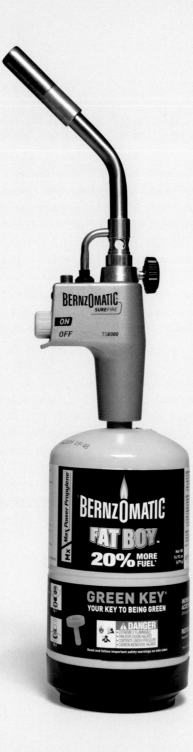

SOLDERING TORCH

Whether you're sweating pipes, making jewelry, or creating a crème brûlée in the kitchen, a soldering torch is your go-to. Look for a self-lighting option like TurboTorch. This swirl combustion concentrates the flame's heat, reducing brazing time and saving gas. For jewelry and lamp making, you'll need a number of nozzles for directing the flame, from a pinpoint to a wider warming flame. For sweating pipes, one good nozzle is all you really need.

Sweating a pipe is a lot like house painting: it's all about the prep. Once the pipe is cut to length using a tube cutter, clean the pipe ends and remove the burrs and any oxidation. Use a clean piece of sandpaper on the outside and a stiff wire brush on the inside.

Brush some plumbing flux on the abraded surfaces and assemble the joint.

Fire up the torch and move the flame around the joint to heat it evenly. When sweating a copper pipe, it will first get shiny as the flux melts, but then it will dull. When this happens, apply the solder: move the flame away from the joint and not near anything combustible, and apply the lead-free solder to the joint. The solder will wick in, and you should have a smooth run of solder surrounding the joint. While the pipe is still warm, apply some flux and wipe the joint thoroughly with a clean rag.

Lead-free solder is used for water supply lines, but it isn't your only choice. Tin/lead solders are also called soft solders. The higher the tin content, the greater the tensile and shear strength of the joint. When there's a higher lead content, the joint cools more slowly and the solder can be worked into the joint for a smoother appearance.

TAP

If the world were a perfect place, the threads for metal parts would never strip, become rusty, or get clogged with dirt, paint, or who knows what else. But that's not the case. Threaded fasteners must fit into threaded holes, and it's not unusual for the threads to become dulled, damaged, or clogged.

The tool that puts metal-fastening threads into a hole is called a tap. This is an extremely hard piece of tool steel that's always harder than the metal that will receive the threads. Thus, the tap literally cuts its way into a well-lubricated hole, leaving a helix-shaped thread in its wake. You use a tap to clean out or otherwise restore the crisp profile of a damaged hole, or you can use it to cut perfect, new threads into a hole that hasn't been tapped.

Some taps are turned using a special T-shaped handle called a tap wrench that's rotated carefully by hand. Others are meant to fit into a cordless drill or a machine tool, like a lathe. Taps come in sizes to match typical bolts, machine screws, and plumbing parts. The tap will have nomenclature like this: ¼-20. In tap speak, that's a quarter twenty. This means it fits a ¼-inch bolt with twenty threads per inch. Whatever the thread, there's a tap to make it.

★ **WISH LIST**

NORSEMAN DRILL AND TOOL MAGNUM SUPER PREMIUM TAP/DRILL SET

Norseman Drill & Tool makes a set of U.S.-manufactured taps and matching drill bits to the highest industry standards, suitable for aerospace metal working. As such, it puts machine shop quality drilling and tapping into the hands of any metal worker, whether professional or amateur. It may be expensive, but it's far superior to run-of-the-mill drills and taps you'll find at your local hardware store.

TONGUE AND GROOVE PLIERS

Howard Manning, chief engineer for the Champion DeArment Tool Company, invented tongue and groove pliers in 1933, improving on standard designs by adding length and leverage and increasing the jaw width. The new tool caught on among car mechanics, who used it to repair water pumps.

In 1953, the company's engineers redesigned the tongue and groove, undercutting the tongue to give the tool a firmer bite—a tweak that prevents it from slipping and busting your knuckles. They've made other improvements over the years, but the instantly recognizable grip color—probably the only hand tool color ever trademarked—has remained the same.

"Back in the early 1950s, all the pliers manufacturers started putting colored PVC (polyvinyl chloride) on their grips," says Bill DeArment, great-grandson of the company's founder. Crescent chose red; STANLEY, yellow. DeArment's father and uncle picked a beautiful sky blue that no one else had—and the company has used that color since 1956. In 1962, Champion changed its name to Channellock; DeArment is the president and CEO. And today, tongue and groove pliers are an essential for mechanics, farmers, plumbers, and average Joes everywhere.

TIP!

GET TWO
These irreplaceable pliers are the first tool plumbers reach for when they need to grab, pull, twist, hold, tighten, or loosen something. We suggest getting two different sizes so you're ready for anything: a 10-inch and a 12-inch.

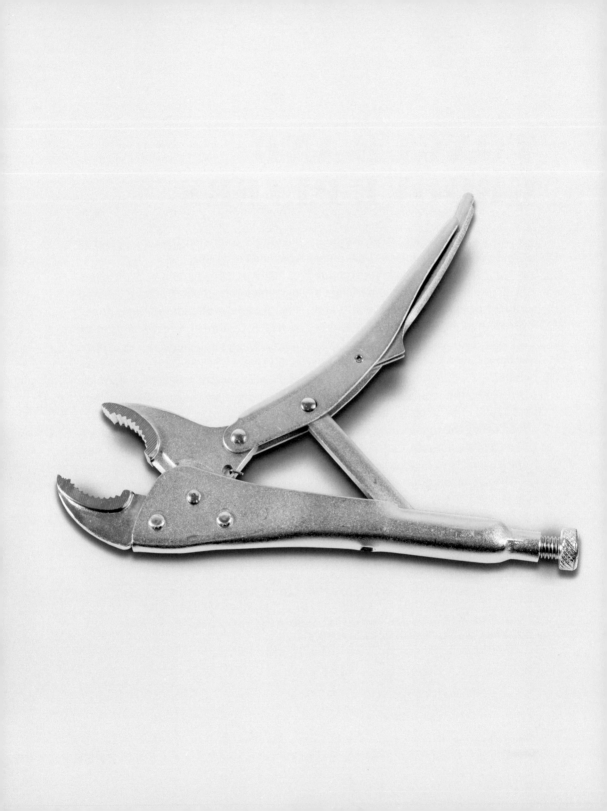

VISE-GRIP

Vise-Grips, also called locking pliers, are considered by many to be the very first hybrid tool. Patented in 1924 by inventor and blacksmith William Petersen, they're part pliers and part vise. Petersen realized his job as a blacksmith would be easier if he had a set of pliers that would clamp down and hold his workpiece in a vise-like grip. After experimenting with several prototypes, he developed the screw mechanism in the handle to adjust the opening of the pliers and, a few years later, developed the locking handle.

The tool was popular among farmers and mechanics in Petersen's area of Nebraska. Although the Great Depression slowed his new company's growth, his small manufacturing plant was staffed by nearly forty employees. By 1941, the little plant was operating at full capacity.

Defense industries building ships and aircraft used thousands of these handy tools. Some shipbuilders, who were strapped for time, actually welded the vise-grips into the hull of their ships. After the war, Petersen took advantage of the first National Hardware Show in 1945, where the tool was billed as the "World's Most Versatile Hand Tool."

The original tool came with a wire-cutting option, which is still available. Now the tool comes in a variety of shapes and sizes. The familiar round nose pliers with four points of contact on bolts are still the most common and widely recognized version. There are also needle-nose and straight-jawed models, as well as specialized sheet metal–working pliers. One of the more significant and recent improvements has to be the soft grip, which is a real bonus when you're working out in the cold.

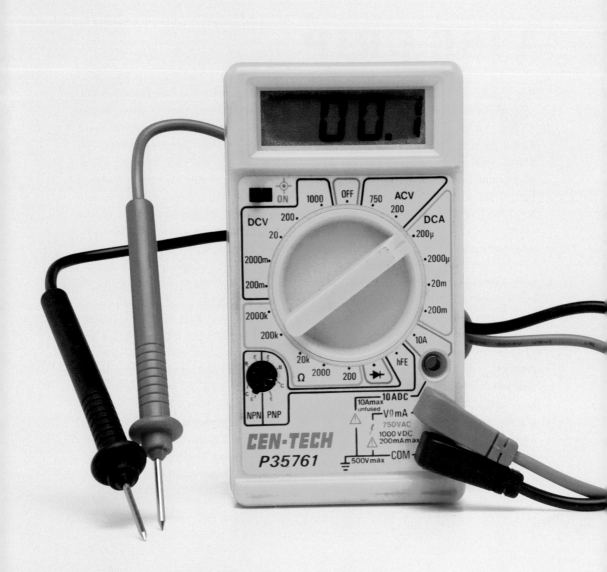

VOLT/OHM METER

While water seeks to fill space, electricity searches for a conductor. You're able to see when a faucet isn't delivering water or when a drain works slowly—but it's simply not possible to see where electricity is flowing. That's why it's crucial to have a volt/ohm meter, often called a multimeter, in your toolbox.

This tool is far more versatile than its two-part name suggests. Aside from measuring voltage and resistance (ohms), it also measures current flow (amperage) and often can emit a tone to indicate a complete circuit (continuity).

There are two types of multimeters. An analog meter is generally less expensive and has a pointer that moves across a printed scale to indicate ohms, amperage, continuity, and so on. However, its functionality is limited by the width of the scale's pointer and its range. Accuracy can also be problematic, compromised by vibrations, precision printing on the labels, the lack of calibrations, and errors introduced because of nonhorizontal use of the mechanical display. Analog volt/ohm meters typically measure within 3-percent accuracy, which may not be precise enough for your needs—certainly not if you're trying to diagnose electrical problems in your car by tracing voltage drops.

We recommend purchasing a more expensive digital meter, which will run you a few hundred dollars and will reliably provide you with a digital readout accurate to 0.5 percent on the DC voltage ranges. It's unlikely you'll need a Category IV meter (used to measure house meters), so look for a Category III if you'll be testing appliance outlets or distribution panels. Always check your meter's specific measuring range before using it.

WIRE STRIPPER

One of the most basic and profoundly important tools in an electrician's tool kit—other than a voltage detector or multimeter—is a proper wire stripper (also called an electrician's multitool). It strips wire, crimps connections, and cuts electrical screws. It can be used on house wiring, but it also works on electronics projects, low-voltage wiring for doorbells, yard lighting, automotive work, and appliance repair.

Why is the tool so important? In order to make an electrical connection, the insulation needs to be removed from wire without damaging the wire itself. If you're working on stranded wire, you don't want to remove any of the strands in the process of stripping away the insulation sheath. This makes the wire smaller than it was designed to be—and that's an electrical hazard. If you're working with solid copper wire, you don't want to damage the copper. A nick will conduct electricity less efficiently and, in the worst case, may be a stress area that can heat up and burn through.

More elaborate wire strippers have a series of holes for cutting electrical screws to length. These screws have a very fine thread, and they are easily damaged if you try to cut them by other means. Finally, the base or front of the tool will have crimping dies. There are many instances in electrical work, whether it's home wiring, auto repair, repairing outdoor power equipment, electronics work, or appliance repair, when you'll need to attach a crimp fitting onto the wire's end. Known as a wiring termination, this fitting may be a slide-on fitting that attaches to another fitting, or it may be a ring terminal that receives an electrical screw or fits over a battery post. It's important that a crimp fitting be tightly attached to the wire without damaging it.

PROJECT ▼

① ②

How to Wire a Light Switch

A simple single-pole light switch will run you just a few bucks, making it one of the least expensive building components to replace. So if you have switches that are old and discolored, were broken by someone moving a heavy piece of furniture, or are just plain worn-out, then there's no reason not to fix them. The swap-out takes only 15 minutes, and you can handle the job even if you've never done basic electrical work before.

Instructions

1. **SAFETY FIRST:** Turn off the electrical circuit where you plan to work by throwing the appropriate switch on the circuit breaker. Then remove the switch cover plate. But don't take it for granted that the circuit is dead. Using a non-contact voltage tester, probe around the wires on the switch and inside the box. The tester should not light or beep.

   Now pull the switch forward and out of the box, and use the detector to search for other live wires. Everything in that box should be dead. If so, you're ready to proceed. If not, it means someone used that box to make a connection to another electrical circuit on a different circuit breaker. It's not a common problem, but with old houses, anything's possible. We opened an old switch box once and found half the downstairs circuits were connected in that one box—an expensive problem to solve.

2. **GET STARTED:** If the wiring in the box is dead and nothing appears out of the ordinary, loosen each terminal screw and remove the hooked wire from beneath the screwhead. Take off the switch and bend each wire out of the way. Vacuum out the box if it's dirty.

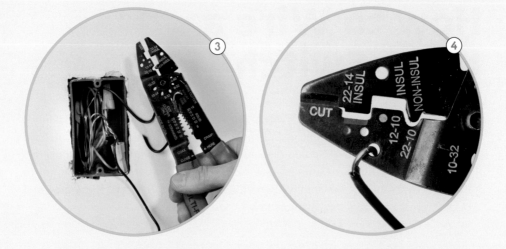

(③) **CLIP AND STRIP:** Check the ends of the wires for rough or nicked spots. Remember, wires expand and contract slightly with every use cycle and can eventually fail at these stress points. Clip off the damaged area and carefully strip about ½ inch of insulation to expose pristine wire.

(④) **BEND A HOOK:** Insert the wire into one of the holes at the tip of an electrician's multitool. Bend the copper into a rounded hook. You can also use a pair of needle-nose pliers to bend a neat hook in the conductors.

KNOW WHEN TO ASK FOR HELP
If you find other electrical problems like burned wires, frayed wires, or signs of shoddy workmanship, stop what you're doing and call an electrician to take over. Why? You never know if you're looking at isolated damage or the tip of an iceberg. A seasoned electrician will know what to look for and how to snoop for other problems.

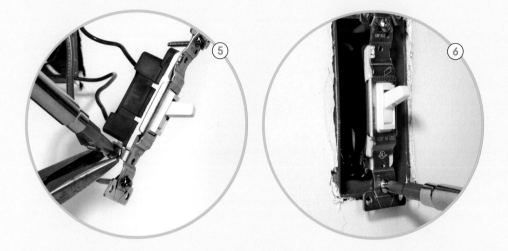

⑤ ATTACH WIRES: Position the switch so it's on when its lever is up. Attach the power wires to the brass terminal screws so the rounded hooks point clockwise. Attach a grounding wire to the green screw in the same manner, with a clockwise bend and direction. Remember that the grounding-screw tab is delicate. Grip it with needle-nose pliers as you tighten the screw.

⑥ INSTALL THE NEW SWITCH: There's an extra-measure of protection that's useful if the switch is located inside a metal box. After the switch is wired, wrap electrical tape around its body and terminal screws to shield live electrical terminals from the metal box body. This isn't called for in the National Electrical Code, but it's not a bad idea, especially in the small crowded electrical boxes found in old homes. If the box is a modern plastic type with plastic-sheathed wiring, you can skip this step.

Screw the switch to the box and mount the cover plate over the switch. Restore power to the circuit by switching the circuit breaker back on, and test the switch. It should work properly, and your work is done.

A

Adhesives, 8–9
Adjustable wrench, 177
Air compressor, 179
Allen (hex) wrenches, 181
Angle grinder, 183
Awl, 91

B

Ball-peen hammer, 185
Bar clamp, 93
Bench plane, 95
Beveling with handsaws, 99
Block plane, 97
Bluestone patio, building,
    169–173
Bow rake, 143
Bow saw, 145
Bricks. See Concrete and bricks
Bucket, five-gallon, 8

C

Carpenter's square, 17
Caulk gun, 101
Caulking, 101
C clamp, 99
Center punch, 187
Chain saw, 147
Chalk line, 19
Chisels
    about: to have in toolbox,
        189
    cold, 189
    mason's, 59
    wood, 133
Chop saw, 113
Clamps
    about: protecting clamped
        surfaces, 131
    bar clamp, 93
    C clamp, 99
    fact-action clamp, 109
    spring clamp, 131
    wooden cam clamp, 109
Claw hammer, 23
Cold chisel, 189
Combination square, 25
Combination wrench, 191

Concrete and bricks
    about: plugging chisel, 59;
        removing ivy from bricks, 153
    brick trowel, 15
    finishing trowel, 27
    float, 29
    mason's chisel, 59
Construction tools, 11–83
    about: lubrication for big
        cutting jobs, 13; making
        improvised rubber mallet,
        23; plugging chisel, 59
    benchtop table saws, 13
    brick trowel, 15
    carpenter's square, 17
    chalk line, 19
    circular saw, 21
    claw hammer, 23
    combination square, 25
    concrete-finishing trowel, 27
    concrete float, 29
    cordless drill, 31
    drywall knife, 33
    drywall saw, 35
    drywall square, 37
    earmuffs, 39
    extension cord, 41
    extension ladder, 43
    flashlight, 45
    gooseneck (wrecking) bar, 47
    hole saw, 49
    impact driver, 51
    jigsaw, 53
    laser level, 55
    level, 57
    mason's chisel, 59
    nail apron/tool bag, 61
    plumb bob, 63
    reciprocating saw, 65
    safety glasses/goggles, 67
    saw horses, 69
    shop vacuum, 71
    sledgehammer, 73
    snips, 75
    speed square, 77
    stepladders, 79
    tape measure, 81
    utility knife, 83

Coping saw, 103
Cordless drill, 31
Cord wrappers, 85
Crescent wrench, 177
Crosscut saw, 105
Cup plunger, 193
Cutters, pipe and tubing, 211

D

Die, tap and, 195, 223
Drain clogs, avoiding/unclogging,
    215
Drill bits, 197
Drills and drilling. See also Die,
    tap and
    about: sharpening bits, 197
    bits for, 197
    center punch for starting holes
        in metal, 187
    cordless drill, 31
    impact driver, 51
    pocket hole jig, 119
Dropped valuables, retrieving,
    72
Drywall
    about: fixing seasonal cracks,
        33
    knife, 33
    saw, 35
    square, 37
Duct tape, 8
Dust mask, 107

E

Earmuffs and ear protection
    importance, 39
Electrical tools and processes
    about: fish tape alternative, 199;
        when to ask for help, 234
    extension cord, 41
    fish tape, 199
    how to wire light switches,
        233–235
    volt/ohm meter, 229
    wire stripper, 231
Extension cord, 41
Extension ladder, 43
Eye protection, 67

Index

F

Fact-action clamp, 109
Farmhouse table, making, 135–139
File (metal) and filing, 205
Fire extinguisher, 7
First aid kit, 7
Fish tape, 199
5-in-1 Tool, 89
Flashlight, 45

G

Garbage can, making, 27
Garden trowel, 149
Glasses, safety, 67
Glue, 8–9
Gooseneck (wrecking) bar, 47
Grinder, angle, 183

H

Hacksaw, 201
Hammers
    about: making improvised
        rubber mallet, 23
    ball-peen, 185
    claw, 23
    sledgehammer, 73
Handles (riveted), fixing, 149
Handles (shovel), replacing, 165
Hand truck, 151
Hex wrenches, 181
Hole saw, 49

I

Impact driver, 51

K

Knives
    about: how to sharpen, 127
    sharpening stones for, 127
    utility knife, 83

L

Ladders
    about: combination ladder, 43
    extension ladder, 43
    stepladders, 79

Landscaping tools, 141–167
    about: building a bluestone
        patio with, 169–173;
        how to trim trees, 159;
        removing ivy from bricks,
        153; replacing shovel
        handles, 165
    bow rake, 143
    bow saw, 145
    chain saw, 147
    garden trowel, 149
    hand truck, 151
    loppers, 153
    pick axe, 155
    post-hole digger, 157
    pruner, 159
    rope, 161
    round nose shovel, 163
    square nose shovel, 165
    wheelbarrow, 167
Laser level, 55
Leaf rake, 143
Levels
    about: preventing slippage
        of, 57
    laser level, 55
    types and sizes, 57
Lighting. See also Electrical tools
        and processes
    building basic work light, 45
    flashlight, 45
    how to wire light switches,
        233–235
Linesman pliers, 217
Locking pliers, 227
Loppers, 153
Lube, spray, 9

M

Machinist vise, 203
Marking gauge, 111
Mason's chisel, 59
Measuring tape, 81
Mechanical tools, 175–231
    about: making improvised
        pipe wrench, 213; using
        adjustable wrenches,
        177

    adjustable (crescent) wrench,
        177
    air compressor, 179
    Allen (hex) wrenches, 181
    Angle grinder, 183
    ball-peen hammer, 185
    center punch, 187
    cold chisel, 189
    combination wrench, 191
    cup plunger, 193
    die, 195
    drill bits, 197
    fish tape, 199
    hacksaw, 201
    machinist vise, 203
    metal file, 205
    multibit screwdriver, 207
    needle-nose pliers, 209
    pipe and tubing cutters, 211
    pipe wrench, 213
    plumber's snake, 215
    side-cutting pliers, 217
    socket wrench, 219
    soldering torch, 221
    tap, 223
    tongue and groove pliers, 225
    Vise-Grip, 227
    volt/ohm meter, 229
    wire stripper, 231
Metal snips, 75
Metalworking tools.
        See Mechanical tools
Miter saw, 113
Multibit screwdriver, 207
Multimeter, 229

N

Nail apron, 61
Nails
    nail set, 115
    protecting wall when removing,
        121
    starting using one hand, 37
    types of, 9

O

Ohm/volt meter, 229

P

Painting
about: keeping rollers from drying out, 117
5-in-1 tool, 89
paintbrush/roller, 117
Patio (bluestone), building, 169–173
Pick axe, 155
Pipe and tubing cutters, 211
Pipes, repairing/replacing, 195
Planes
bench, 95
block, 97
shoulder, 129
Pliers
about: recommended for toolbox, 209
locking (Vise-Grip), 227
needle-nose, 209
side-cutting/linesman, 217
tongue and groove, 225
Plumb bob, 63
Plumbing tools. *See* Mechanical tools
Plungers, 193
Pocket hole jig, 119
Post-hole digger, 157
Projects
building bluestone patio, 169–173
farmhouse table, 135–139
wiring light switches, 233–235
worksite essentials (work triangles, cord wrapper, sandpaper ripper), 85
Pruning tools. *See* Landscaping tools
Pry bar, 47
Putty knives
about: how to protect wall with, 121
5-in-1 tool, 89
putty knife, 121

R

Rakes, 143
Random orbital sander, 123
Reciprocating saw, 65

Riveted handles, fixing, 149
Rope, 161
Round nose shovel, 163
Router, 125
Rubber mallet, improvised, 23

S

Safety equipment
dust mask, 107
earmuffs, 39
fire extinguisher, 7
first aid kit, 7
safety glasses/goggles, 67
Sanding
about: making flexible sanding block, 129
random orbital sander for, 123
sandpaper for, 8, 123
Sandpaper ripper, 85
Saw horses, 69
Saws, manual
about: beveling with a handsaw, 99; how to cope, 103
bow saw, 145
coping saw, 103
crosscut saw, 105
drywall saw, 35
hacksaw, 201
Saws, power
about: lubrication for big cutting jobs, 13; steering jigsaws, 53
benchtop table saws, 13
chain saw, 147
circular saw, 21
hole saw, 49
jigsaw, 53
miter saw, 113
reciprocating saw, 65
Scrapers, 89
Screwdriver, multibit, 207
Screws, 9
Screws, making marking gauge with, 111
Sharpening
drill bits, 197
knives, 127
stones for, 127

Shop vacuum, 71
Shoulder plane, 129
Shovels
about: long-handles and D-handles, 163; replacing handles, 165
garden trowel, 149
round nose, 163
square nose, 165
Side-cutting pliers, 217
Sledgehammer, 73
Snake, plumber's, 215
Snips, 75
Socket wrench, 219
Soldering torch, 221
Speed square, 77
Spray lube, 9
Spring clamp, 131
Square nose shovel, 165
Squares
carpenter's, 17
combination, 25
drywall, 37
speed, 77
Stepladders, 79
Supplies, 8–9

T

Table (farmhouse), making, 135–139
Tap, die and, 195, 223
Tape and adhesives, 8–9
Tape measure, 81
Thatch rake, 143
Tongue and groove pliers, 225
Tool bag, 61
Tools
by category. *See* Construction tools; Landscaping tools; Mechanical tools; Woodworking tools
fixing riveted handles, 149
gift hint idea, 9
safety equipment and, 7
supplies and, 8–9
this book and, 5, 6–7, 9
Torch, soldering, 221
Triangles, making, 85

Index

Trowels
  brick trowel, 15
  concrete-finishing trowel, 27
  garden trowel, 149
Tubing cutters, 211
Two-wheel hand truck, 151

U
Utility knife, 83

V
Vacuum, shop, 71
Vise, 203
Vise-Grip, 227
Volt/ohm meter, 229

W
Wheelbarrow, 167
Wire stripper, 231
Wooden cam clamp, 109
Woodworking tools, 87–133
  about: making farmhouse table with, 135–139; making flexible sanding block, 129; making work triangles, cord wrapper, sandpaper ripper with, 85; protecting clamped surfaces, 131; wooden cam clamps, 109
  5-in-1 tool, 89
  awl, 91
  bar clamp, 93
  bench plane, 95
  block plane, 97
  caulk gun, 101
  C clamp, 99
  coping saw, 103
  crosscut saw, 105
  dust mask, 107
  fact-action clamp, 109
  marking gauge, 111
  miter saw, 113
  nail set, 115
  paintbrush/roller, 117
  pocket hole jig, 119
  putty knife, 121
  random orbital sander, 123
  router, 125
  sharpening stones, 127
  shoulder plane, 129
  spring clamp, 131
  wood chisel, 133
Work triangles, making, 85
Wrecking bar, 47
Wrenches
  about: making improvised pipe wrench, 213; using adjustable wrenches, 177
  adjustable (crescent) wrench, 177
  Allen (hex) wrenches, 181
  combination wrench, 191
  pipe wrench, 213
  socket wrench, 219

Photo Credits

HEARSTBOOKS

An Imprint of Sterling Publishing Co., Inc.
1166 Avenue of the Americas
New York, NY 10036

ISBN 978-1-61837-292-5

Distributed in Canada by Sterling Publishing Co., Inc.
c/o Canadian Manda Group, 664 Annette Street
Toronto, Ontario M6S 2C8, Canada
Distributed in the United Kingdom by GMC Distribution Services
Castle Place, 166 High Street, Lewes, East Sussex BN7 1XU, England
Distributed in Australia by NewSouth Books
University of New South Wales, Sydney, NSW 2052, Australia

For information about custom editions, special sales, and premium and corporate purchases,
please contact Sterling Special Sales at 800-805-5489 or specialsales@sterlingpublishing.com.

Manufactured in China

2 4 6 8 10 9 7 5 3 1

sterlingpublishing.com
popularmechanics.com

Cover design by David Ter-Avanesyan
Cover photo retouching by Daniel J. Rutkowski
Interior design by Zachary Gilyard
Photography credits on page 239